Martin

Luther

King, Jr.

Martin
Luther
King, Jr.

ADAM FAIRCLOUGH

The University of Georgia Press ATHENS & LONDON

© 1990, 1995 by Adam Fairclough
Athens, Georgia 30602

Designed by Kathi L. Dailey
Set in Linotype Walbaum by
Tseng Information Systems, Inc.
Printed and bound by Thomson-Shore, Inc.
The paper in this book meets the guidelines for
permanence and durability of the Committee on
Production Guidelines for Book Longevity of the
Council on Library Resources.

Printed in the United States of America

99   98   97   96   95   C   5   4   3   2   1

99   98   97   96   95   P   5   4   3   2   1

Library of Congress Cataloging in Publication Data

Fairclough, Adam.
Martin Luther King, Jr. / Adam Fairclough.
p.   cm.
Includes bibliographical references (p.) and index.
ISBN 0-8203-1690-3 (alk. paper). —
ISBN 0-8203-1653-9 (pbk. : alk. paper)
1. King, Martin Luther, Jr., 1929–1968.
2. Afro-Americans—Biography.   3. Civil rights
workers—United States—Biography.
4. Baptists—United States—Clergy—Biography.   I. Title.
E185.97.K5F35   1995
323'.092—dc20
[B]   94-4171

British Library Cataloging in Publication Data available

To Connie

Contents

Martin
Luther
King, Jr.

1

The Shaping of a Mind

MARTIN LUTHER KING, JR., was born on January 15, 1929, in Atlanta, Georgia. On April 4, 1968, a white man shot and killed him in Memphis, Tennessee; he was only thirty-nine when he died. King's public career spanned less than thirteen years, but during that time, from 1956 to 1968, he became the most popular and effective leader of the civil rights movement in America, and emerged on the international stage as a forceful and eloquent proponent of nonviolence. Showered with awards and prizes, including the Nobel Peace Prize, King attained a position of prestige and influence unprecedented for an African American. Moreover, he still casts a long shadow. His assassination transformed him into a martyr, and in 1985 Congress added his birthday to the list of national holidays, placing King in the same league as George Washington and Abraham Lincoln. Although it is more than a quarter of a century after his death, King's name and image are ubiquitous. Thousands of streets, schools, and public buildings commemorate his memory. His portrait adorns the homes of millions of African Americans. His name is respected throughout the world; his example is an inspiration to oppressed peoples.

Such recognition obscures another fact about King's life and symbolism, however: although he was a hero to blacks, King incurred the hatred of a great number of whites. Many whites in the South had few good words for King while he lived and shed no tears for him when he died. Fighting to preserve a racially segregated society based on the principle of white supremacy, they mobilized the full resources of the state in an effort to silence him and to crush the civil rights movement. Although finally compelled through federal law to dismantle the structure of white supremacy, their acceptance of desegregation never amounted to more than reluctant acquiescence. Few acknowledged the justice of King's cause or the legitimacy of his methods; many openly gloated over his death.

It seemed that whites in the northern states were more divided in their attitudes. Many—often described as "white liberals"—disapproved of the South's open racism and assisted the civil rights movement with money, moral support, and political pressure. Some of King's most ardent admirers could be found in the white churches and universities of the North. For other whites, however, King's insistence upon racial integration evoked varying degrees of unease and hostility. The "white ethnics" of the northern cities—the descendants of poverty-stricken immigrants who had worked their way up in the most difficult circumstances—were not inclined to sympathize with blacks. They regarded blacks as a threat to their jobs, schools, communities, and physical safety. When King took his movement to Chicago in 1966, he encountered unyielding resistance and naked prejudice.

The attitude of the federal government reflected these conflicting feelings. Outwardly, it sympathized with black aspirations for equality and treated King with respect. Yet Washington did little to aid the civil rights movement until pressure compelled it to act, and the government viewed King with suspicion. President Kennedy feared that King was being influenced by Communists and kept him at arm's length. President Johnson distrusted King's judgment and came to regard him as a political foe. The head of the FBI, J. Edgar Hoover, viewed King as a threat to national security. Even the Supreme Court, the branch of government most sympathetic to the civil rights movement, disapproved of his methods and forced him to serve time in a Birmingham, Alabama, jail. After King's death, many members of Congress bitterly opposed proposals to honor his memory with a national holiday. The recognition accorded King, in life and in death, had to be wrested from a reluctant and at times hostile white majority. It measured the collective progress of African Americans.

In 1929, the year of King's birth, African Americans possessed little wealth and less power. The abolition of slavery in 1865 had made blacks legally free, but Emancipation led to shattered hopes and cruel disappointments. Reconstruction, the Republican party's experiment in political and civil equality, failed ingloriously, as many white southerners used all the means at their command, including violence and terrorism, to reestablish their dominance over the former slaves. In 1877, tired of the struggle and persuaded that the ideal of racial equality flew in the face of blacks' "innate" inferiority, the Republicans abandoned Reconstruction. They left the fate of the freedmen in the hands of their former masters.

Between the end of the nineteenth century and World War I, a racial caste system designed to keep the black population in a position of permanent inferiority had been perfected in the South. Blacks were disfranchised and stripped of all political influence. A complex of segregation laws drew a rigid "color line" between the races, assigning blacks to a separate and inferior position. White lawmakers reinforced the caste system by outlawing miscegenation and defining as "Negro" a person with one black great-grandparent or, in the case of several states, any black ancestry whatever. Black schools were rudimentary or nonexistent, and the few state-funded black colleges offered a diet of "industrial education" designed to keep blacks in menial, domestic, and agricultural occupations. "Educate a nigger," the white saying went, "and spoil a good field hand."

The desire to maintain an abundant supply of cheap and pliant black labor lay at the heart of white supremacy. Despite some movement from farm to city, most blacks remained in the old plantation areas of the South's "Black Belt," a giant arc of tobacco, cotton, and sugar-producing land stretching from Virginia to Texas, which still constituted the backbone of the southern economy. Few blacks owned land—unlike Russia's serfs, they had received none upon their emancipation. Most black farmers worked as sharecroppers, tilling a portion of the landlord's plantation. Sharecropping enabled blacks to farm as family units but offered them little real independence or prospect of economic betterment. They remained landless laborers, paid in kind rather than cash, and many were permanently in debt. Living conditions were wretched, often worse than under slavery. In parts of the South sharecropping merged imperceptibly into the illegal but widespread practice of peonage: landlords enslaved black debtors and sometimes killed them if they tried to escape. If black farmers became too prosperous, however, jealous whites sometimes drove them out. Buttressing white supremacy were a double standard of justice, a brutal penal system, and an unwritten rule that permitted and even encouraged "private" violence against blacks. A black corpse dangling from a tree provided the starkest symbol of southern racism. Between 1882 and 1927 whites lynched 3,302 blacks, often in public ceremonies of revolting sadism. Although lynching slowly declined thereafter, it was still frighteningly common when King was growing up.

Looking back on his childhood, Martin Luther King, Jr., recalled a loving family, a close-knit community, and a church that functioned as a second home. This idyllic picture seems in jarring contrast with the realities of black life in the 1930s and 1940s. Despite its comparative youth and reputation for economic progressivism, Atlanta was as rigidly segregated as any southern city and, in some respects, more racist than most. In 1906 blacks in Atlanta suffered an outbreak of white mob violence in one of the South's worst race riots. Atlanta also had the dubious distinction of being birthplace and headquarters of the modern Ku Klux Klan.

Yet King's memory of a happy childhood did not stray far from the truth. In common with other southern cities, Atlanta's black population included a small but prosperous upper class, which contrived to insulate itself from the harsher edges of white supremacy. This "black bourgeoisie" was partly a product of racial segregation, for the imposition of a strict "color line" had encouraged blacks to turn in on themselves, and segregated black neighborhoods required black entrepreneurs and professionals. Atlanta's black community boasted thriving businesses, impressive churches, superior private colleges, a radio station, a daily newspaper, and a rich social network of clubs and organizations. Born into Atlanta's black elite, King always remembered his family and community as sources of emotional strength and stability. "This was a wholesome community," he insisted. "Crime was at a minimum . . . and most of our neighbors were deeply religious." King never experienced economic hardship, and his father, a prominent and well-to-do clergyman, tried to shield his family from the more humiliating aspects of segregation.[1]

Martin Luther King, Sr.—"Daddy" King—was a towering figure in the young King's life and a major influence in shaping his personality. First and foremost, he connected Martin, Jr., to the church, the oldest and most influential black institution. Born in rural Georgia to a family of sharecroppers, Daddy King had moved to Atlanta and in 1926 married the daughter of A. D. Williams, the pastor of Ebenezer Baptist Church and a respected black civic leader. In 1931, upon the Reverend Williams's death, the elder King inherited the pastorate of the church, which had been established in the 1880s and recently rebuilt. Situated on Auburn Avenue, the main thoroughfare of the black business district, Ebenezer was a substantial if plain brick structure that came to boast a congregation several thousand strong. For the young King, Ebenezer united family and community and provided a secure and clearly-defined world; the church was in the blood of this son and grandson of Baptist ministers. "I have never experienced the so-called 'crisis moment,'" he recalled when he was a divinity student. "Conversion for me has been the gradual intaking of the whole ideals set forth in my family and my environment, and I must admit that this intaking has been largely unconscious." Deep roots, a strong sense of identity, and a love of the black church placed him at the heart of Atlanta's black community.

King's father also provided young Martin with a strong role model. Daddy King was a stern disciplinarian with a volcanic temper, imposing his patriarchal authority with the aid of frequently administered corporal punishment. Although Christine, the eldest sibling, seems to have escaped physical chastisement, the two sons, Martin and Alfred Daniel, endured the sting of the switch until their mid-teens. Yet throughout his life King exhibited unabashed respect and affection for his father, eventually joining him as copastor of Ebenezer Baptist Church. In a revealing essay written when he was about twenty, King praised his father as a "real father"—someone who "always put his family first." Glossing over the fact that Daddy King had married into wealth, King stressed his father's capacity for hard work and frugality. "He never wastes his money at the expense of his family," King wrote. "He has always had sense enough not to live beyond his means." And despite his father's harsh discipline, King dwelt on the warm, intimate relationships within the King household. He had been especially fond of his maternal grandmother.

Perhaps these memories were tinged by nostalgia. But it is not difficult to see why King should be impressed and even awed by his father. At a time when whites viewed blacks as feckless and improvident, Daddy King was the epitome of bourgeois virtue. During a period of economic depression when black families were disintegrating under the stress of poverty, he not merely kept his family together but also provided for all their needs. In an age when whites viewed black neighborhoods as hellholes of vice and social disorganization, Daddy King's church stood like an anchor in a stable and respectable community. And in a dominant culture that stereotyped blacks as childish, sycophantic clowns, King's father prided himself on being the equal of any white person. He spoke to whites with blunt candor—once telling a policeman not to call him "boy." In short, Martin Luther King, Sr., was a living contradiction of all that whites expected blacks to be. No wonder his son was proud of him and took the beatings in stride. "I guess the influence of my father had a great deal to do with my going into the ministry," he confessed. "My admiration for him was the great moving factor; he set forth a noble example I didn't mind following."

The younger King also inherited his father's—and indeed his grandfather's—social and political concerns. A. D. Williams had been a founder and early president of the Atlanta branch of the National Association for the Advancement of Colored People (NAACP). He had led protests against racial discrimination, campaigned for black public schools, and pushed for black voter registration. Daddy King took an equally broad view of his pastoral role, and soon came to see himself as a leader of Atlanta's black community. He helped to organize voter registration drives, sat on the board of Morehouse College, and involved himself in the NAACP. While no radical, he rejected the divide between religion and politics. King, Sr., gave his son an appreciation of the struggles of earlier generations of African Americans. He saw a

basic continuity in black history and refused to join in the fashion-
able denunications of such past leaders as Booker T. Washington.

If the church was King's second home, preaching was his first
and lifelong love. Long before he became an ordained minister, King had absorbed the styles and techniques of the black
preacher. He had spent many hours of his childhood and adoles-
cence listening to his father, to guest preachers at Ebenezer, and
to William Holmes Borders, a black minister who pastored Wheat
Street Baptist Church a few blocks away. King's love of oratory
first won him public notice at the tender age of fifteen, when he
won a public-speaking competition with a speech entitled, "The
Negro and the Constitution." Even then he was linking oratory
with the struggle against racial discrimination. "Black America
still wears chains," he declaimed. "The finest Negro is at the
mercy of the meanest white man."

King learned more than technique, therefore, when he became
a preacher; he also inherited a theology of freedom that went
back to slavery days. From the time that slaves first converted
to Christianity, blacks had evolved a distinctive interpretation of
the gospel that emphasized the common humanity of all peoples
and their equality in the eyes of God. In the antebellum South,
when the law forbade whites to teach slaves to read and write,
illiterate slave preachers became renowned for the power of their
eloquence; after slavery, spellbinding sermons remained central
to black church services. Through their preaching, ministers gave
black people confirmation of their own worth and the promise
of delivery from oppression. The words and images contained
in the black preaching tradition gave black people a common
language—the basis for a collective racial identity and a shared
yearning for freedom. When he became involved in the civil rights
movement, King's mastery of that common language enabled him
to communicate with ordinary people far more effectively than
secular black leaders had been able to do. King the civil rights

leader was thus a product, above all, of the black church. And his father personified what was best in that church.

Gradually, almost imperceptibly, King moved out of his father's shadow and established his intellectual and emotional independence. His "adolescent identity crisis" entailed no spectacular act of overt rebellion: it was an extended period of doubt and questioning. The process included rejection of some of his father's values. Although proud of Daddy King's worldly success, King came to question the acquisitive individualism that characterized Atlanta's black upper class. Growing up in the depths of the Great Depression, the young boy witnessed harrowing scenes of physical and mental suffering. He asked his parents about the breadlines, but the answers, it seems, did not satisfy him. "I could never get out of my mind the economic insecurity of many of my playmates and the tragic poverty of those living around me." Later, as a college student, vacation jobs brought him into contact with white workers, making him realize "that the poor white was exploited just as much as the Negro." By the late 1940s King had become convinced that rank injustice lurked within the American economic system, and in a student essay spoke of his "anti capitalistic feelings." years later, Daddy King recalled political arguments: "There were some sharp exchanges; I may even have raised my voice a few times." In contrast with his father, who accumulated extensive business interests, King exhibited little interest in acquiring wealth.[2]

King's ideological growth also caused him to question the church. Daddy King automatically assumed that both his sons would enter the ministry and that the elder would eventually succeed to the pastorate of Ebenezer. At about the age of twelve, however, King began to profess doubts about religion, and when he entered Atlanta's Morehouse College at the age of fifteen, he toyed with the idea of a career in law or medicine. As biographer Stephen Oates has argued, on one level King was rebelling in "subtle, indirect ways" against his father. On another level, however, King's growing social awareness and intellectual maturity made it quite natural for him to query the church. While black ministers were influential figures, they did not, by and large, take the lead in challenging the racial caste system. As Daddy King recalled, "Instead of championing the rights of their members, a lot of these ministers simply took their orders from whites and passed them along to Negroes. And the message was simply one of accommodation and silence." In the 1930s African-American intellectuals were lambasting the church for encouraging blacks to accept the status quo and find solace in emotional mumbo jumbo; many scorned ministers as parasitic Uncle Toms who collaborated with the white oppressors. The young King—in his own words, "the questioning and precocious type"—wanted the church to be more politically engaged and less oriented toward empty emotionalism.[3]

It was at Morehouse College that King's inherited religious beliefs acquired the kind of philosophical and theological content that enabled him to conquer his doubts about the ministry. Founded by the white Baptist church shortly after the Civil War, Morehouse shone like a beacon of academic excellence among the segregated black colleges of the South, nurturing a potent combination of moral integrity, intellectual inquiry, and civic responsibility. The Morehouse ethos bore the impress of the college president, Dr. Benjamin Mays, a remarkable man who influenced generations of black students. Mays was an outspoken critic of the obscurantism, over-emotionalism, and poor training of most black pastors. In an important sociological study of the black church, he lamented the fact that even in the depths of the depression few clergymen referred to social and economic issues, relying instead on rambling, illogical, "shouting" sermons that dwelt almost exclusively on the life hereafter. If the church were to retain its status as the cornerstone of black life, Mays insisted, it needed educated ministers who would adapt the Christian message to modern realities, addressing the pressing worldly concerns of ordinary blacks. George D. Kelsey, a professor of religion, likewise hammered home the need for a socially relevant, intellectually coherent ministry. "The shackles of fundamentalism were removed from my body," King recalled. In a sense, Mays and Kelsey merely confirmed what King had already learned from his father.[4]

At the age of nineteen, recently ordained and with a degree in sociology from Morehouse, King began three years of study at Crozer Theological Seminary in Chester, Pennsylvania, leading to a bachelor's degree in divinity. At Crozer he gave a radical edge to the values imparted by Mays and Kelsey by absorbing the evangelical liberalism of Dr. George W. Davis, who introduced King to the ideas of Walter Rauschenbusch, the principal exponent of the early twentieth-century Social Gospel movement. An outspoken critic of industrial capitalism, Rauschenbusch urged the church to confront social evil and to work toward a kind of Christian socialism, striving for a "Kingdom of God" on earth.

King's study of Marx also struck a sympathetic chord. Untouched by the revisionism of the Frankfurt school, and echoing the textbook definitions of the day, King deplored Marxism for substituting materialism for religious and spiritual values, and for utilizing ruthless methods that led to "strangulating totalitarianism." Even so, he applauded Marx for exposing the injustices of capitalism, promoting class consciousness among the workers, and challenging the complacency of the Christian churches. In spite of the developing cold war, an atmosphere that discouraged criticism of free enterprise, King became convinced that capitalism had "failed to meet the needs of the masses" and had "outlived its usefulness."[5]

During his final year at Crozer, King studied the Protestant theologian Reinhold Niebuhr, whose writings reflected the disillusionment—so common after the carnage of the Great War—with Victorian ideas of progress. In his influential book *Moral*

Man and Immoral Society, published in 1932, Niebuhr dismissed the notion that ethics and reason could promote a higher social morality. Individuals might have the capacity for moral improvement, but social groups—particularly classes and nations—developed ideologies that magnified man's natural egoism, hypocrisy, and capacity for self-deception. Utopian schemes for perfecting human society were thus doomed to failure, Niebuhr believed, and might even displace current evils with worse ones. By the same token, it was futile for oppressed groups to appeal to the reason or altruism of ruling elites: imperialism, territorial aggression, and class exploitation could be combatted only by means of force, whether in the form of revolution, political power, or war—even Gandhi's form of nonviolence embodied coercion. Niebuhr's powerful analysis was perfectly attuned to the age of ideology, and was rendered prophetic by the failure of the League of Nations, the horrors of Hitler and Stalin, and the emergence of the cold war.

Perhaps the most valuable experience that King had at Crozer was social rather than intellectual: it was the first time that he had lived in an integrated social setting for any length of time. Crozer had gone out of its way to recruit black students, and King found that blacks made up a third of his class. His classmates also included foreigners of half a dozen nationalities as well as a sprinkling of southern whites. "No major seminary of any denomination had achieved such a racial mix," writes King biographer Taylor Branch. For King, the experience was a happy one; he made white friends and fell in love with a young white woman. For the rest of his life, King never wavered in the belief that integration brought out the best in people and enriched their lives. It certainly did something for King: merely an average student at Morehouse, he graduated from Crozer in 1951 at the top of his class.[6]

At Boston University, studying for a doctorate in the school of theology, King delved more deeply into modern philosophy and theology. He continued to ponder Niebuhr's insistence on the enduring reality of sin and the impossibility of moral certainty. But at Boston he found a theological conception of God that confirmed his own optimism about human progress. King attributed his optimistic outlook to his happy childhood. "It is quite easy for me to think of a God of love mainly because I grew up in a family where love was central and where loving relationships were ever present." Influenced by his teachers at Boston University, he endowed this view with intellectual substance through the philosophy of personalism. God was not a philosophical abstraction or a desperate affirmation of the unknowable, but a "personal spirit, who in love creates, sustains, and orders all." Through religious faith man could become God's coworker, subordinating his innate evil and reinforcing what was best in human personality. King thought Niebuhr's view of human nature too pessimistic, and that it underestimated the human potential for moral improvement. As he was to do throughout his life, King borrowed the concept of the Hegelian dialectic to reconcile schools of thought that on their face were mutually exclusive—simply affirming as truths those ideas with which he agreed.[7]

When King left the university, however, he had yet to resolve the question of how blacks could gain equality. Although Niebuhr had convinced him of the absolute necessity for the use of coercion to restrain evil and combat oppression, he remained unpersuaded of the relevance of Gandhian nonviolence—despite the fact that Niebuhr himself had argued that "non-violence is a particularly strategic instrument for an oppressed group which is hopelessly in the minority." And although King realized that blacks in the United States were so heavily outnumbered that violence was suicidal, he was skeptical of pacifism.[8]

In later years, King referred to his Protestant namesake with great pride. Yet the young Martin Luther King, Jr., was no rebel: on the contrary, in many ways he seemed thoroughly conventional. Accepting discipline and authority had never been a problem for him. Dutiful son, assiduous scholar, model student, jovial companion, he moved through school and college with consummate ease—even if he did plagiarize large chunks of his Ph.D. dissertation. The Bohemian lifestyle exerted no appeal, and he embraced the bourgeois conventions of the time. King "likes good clothes," his earliest biographer noted, "a suite at the Waldorf, dinner at Sardi's, plane trips, long-distance telephone calls, and money in the bank." His attitude toward women would certainly be termed sexist, although at the time his male peers probably considered his behavior conservative. He made it crystal clear to his bride-to-be, Coretta Scott, that he was looking for a pastor's wife, and that she must abandon her plans for a singing career. In King's eyes, the woman's place was most definitely in the home, and her primary role was that of wife and mother.[9]

King's conformity to middle-class values reflected more than his family background or the social mores of the time. In his punctilious manners and exaggerated concern over personal appearance, for example, the smartly dressed young man displayed not merely vanity but also a determined desire to dispel the notion that blacks were always late, usually grinning, and invariably dirty. "I was well aware of the typical white stereotype," he admitted, "and for a while I was terribly conscious of trying to avoid identification with it." Later, in his first book, he urged blacks not to let the side down by giving grist for the racist mill: "Our crime rate is far too high. Our level of cleanliness is far too low. . . . We are too often loud and boisterous, and spend far too much on drink. Even the most poverty-stricken among us can purchase a ten-cent bar of soap." In the presence of whites King displayed—unless he knew them well—studied seriousness and solemn reserve.[10]

Nor was King in any sense a political activist, despite his dissent from capitalist orthodoxy. Too young to be part of the generation that had been politicized by the Southern Negro Youth Congress, he arrived at Crozer when the surge of left-wing radicalism associated with the New Deal and World War II was already in retreat. The intolerant conservatism of cold war anticommunism now set the tone of public life. But King's abstention from politics stemmed more from temperament than from lack of opportunity. He enjoyed his leisure time, and student activism held little attraction. He did not feel moved to join organized protests against Jim Crow, McCarthyism, or the Korean War. Above all, perhaps, King lacked the sense of burning injustice that makes political radicals. Of course, he harbored deep anger over racial discrimination and, as a youth, had been "determined to hate every white person." Friendships with white students, however, enabled him to conquer this hatred and put racism in perspective. Life had been good to him—when he graduated from Crozer his parents gave him a new Chevrolet—and while he had not taken life easily, he did not wish to make it more difficult for himself.[11]

In his marriage and selection of pastorate, King finally established his independence from Daddy King. Yet he did it in such a way as to mollify his father. He knew that it was idle to engage him in argument and that he could best get his way by keeping quiet. Introducing Coretta to his parents for the first time, for example, he sat through an appalling display of bad manners by his father without saying a word. As Coretta put it many years later, "He was amazingly respectful, thoughtful, and considerate of Daddy King's feelings." For all their differences, the son retained, in his own words, "that admiration for a real father." There was, some observers thought, a competitive edge to the relationship. Daddy King, an established and respected figure, seemed to think that his son might be content to play second fiddle to him as copastor of Ebenezer. King, for his part, was determined to be his own man and to equal his father's success.[12]

How did a young man of such broad mental horizons expect to be satisfied with the humdrum life of a Baptist minister in a backwater like Montgomery, Alabama? Reflecting on his decision to accept the pastorate of Dexter Avenue Baptist Church rather than to pursue an academic career, King stressed his feeling of moral obligation to return south, "at least for a few years," in order to serve the people whence he sprang—at Crozer he had ended a relationship with a white woman, realizing that an interracial marriage would make this option impossible. In Montgomery King soon became active in the NAACP and the Alabama Council on Human Relations, a biracial discussion group. He also encouraged his parishioners to become registered voters. But King had not ruled out an eventual return to academic life, and, despite his concern for social uplift, he had no intention of making waves. Settling down into his new career and family— a daughter, Yolanda, was born in 1955—King enjoyed the full social life that went with the job of pastoring one of the oldest and most prestigious black churches in the community. He also honed his preaching skills. As a student at Crozer he had been so intensely intellectual that one pastor, rating King's guest sermon, criticized him for "an attitude of aloofness, disdain and possibly snobbishness." As he grew more self-assured he began to unbend, developing a more intimate, emotional style of preaching.[13]

Nobody expected blacks in Montgomery to make history. Most seemed apathetic, and the few activists seemed riven by factionalism and petty rivalries. But anger over the bus situation had simmered below the surface for years. When a well-known and respected black woman, Rosa Parks, refused to surrender her bus seat to a white man on the afternoon of December 1, 1955, she was arrested and taken to jail. A group of black women promptly decided upon a boycott and, running off thousands of leaflets, called upon the black population to stay off the buses. King supported the protest but felt skeptical about its chances of success. But the response of the black community ushered in a new chapter in American history and transformed King's life.

2

The Montgomery Bus Boycott

FEW PRACTICES EVOKED such bitter resentment among African Americans in the South as segregation in public transportation. In theory, the system embodied the principle of "separate but equal," the rule laid down by the Supreme Court in 1896 to square state segregation laws with the ban on racial discrimination contained in the Fourteenth Amendment to the Constitution, passed in 1867. In fact, segregation meant separate and unequal.

The buses in Montgomery, Alabama, reserved the first ten seats for whites and the rear ten seats for blacks. But the back rows were located above the engine, and their occupants had to endure, especially in the summer months, the discomfort of scorching heat. In the middle rows, the driver separated blacks and whites on an ad hoc basis, according to the ratio of one race to the other. But the system meant that in a crowded bus blacks would have to stand even if all ten "white" seats were empty. Moreover, several black passengers might have to surrender their seats in order to accommodate a single white passenger—the law forbade whites and blacks from sitting in the same row. As far back as the 1860s blacks had resisted the introduction of segregated, or

Jim Crow, streetcars by boycotting them. In the early twentieth century, however, the tide of segregation swept across the South, and black protests proved unavailing.

Black distaste for segregation entailed far more than resentment of the discomfort and inconvenience it entailed. African Americans knew perfectly well that whites accepted physical proximity with them when they were cooks, housemaids, farmhands, and servants. Only when physical proximity implied equality of status did whites object. Thus, Jim Crow trains, streetcars, and buses daily reminded blacks of their inferior status; the phrase "back of the bus" became shorthand for racial discrimination.

As blacks migrated to the cities, and as whites switched from public transportation to private cars, black hatred of segregated buses grew apace. Although blacks often comprised a large majority of the regular passengers, the bus companies refused to employ black drivers. And the black riders felt continually humiliated by the manner in which the white drivers enforced the rules—their tone of voice; their use of terms like "boy," "girl," "Auntie," and "nigger"; and their insistence that blacks pay their fare at the front but board the bus at the rear. There were even occasions, especially during the war, when gun-toting drivers shot and killed black passengers.

The fact that blacks in Montgomery decided to boycott the buses was unusual but not unique. Two years earlier, in the city of Baton Rouge, Louisiana, blacks had done precisely that, staying off the buses for a week. There, too, a Baptist clergyman led the protest. The boycott in Montgomery, however, assumed a far larger significance than its obscure precursor in Baton Rouge. This was no seven-day wonder, but a sustained protest the like of which the South had never seen: blacks stayed off the buses in Montgomery for 381 days. And during that time their unity, determination, and élan astonished the world, making the Montgomery bus boycott the concrete symbol of a new spirit of resistance on the part of African Americans in the South. At the end of it, blacks returned to the buses on an integrated basis. And King, initially a self-effacing figurehead, had emerged as a leader of authority and stature, a man with a message for both the South and the nation.

When a group of black ministers met on the afternoon of December 5, 1955, to discuss the day-old bus boycott, they asked King to serve as spokesman for the protest. At first glance, it was a puzzling choice: only twenty-six years old, King had lived in Montgomery less than two years. But at the same time, the selection of King had a certain logic to it. As a fresh face, few people had any objections to him; he had not had time to make enemies. As a new pastor very much absorbed in his family and career, he was not identified with any of the leadership factions that jockeyed for influence within the black community. On a more positive note, King had impressed his congregation by the decisive manner in which he had imposed his authority upon Dexter Avenue Baptist Church, insisting that "Leadership never ascends from the pew to the pulpit, but . . . descends from the pulpit to the pew." King was obviously intelligent and articulate; his credentials were impressive. Above all, the other ministers exhibited a notable lack of enthusiasm for putting their own heads above the parapet. King was the available man.[1]

Preparing to address the first mass meeting of the Montgomery Improvement Association, the organization hastily devised to coordinate the boycott, King worried whether he could rise to the occasion. When he arrived at the meeting place, a church, a thousand people filled every available pew and packed the aisles; several thousand more congregated outside. After a fervent rendition of "Onward Christian Soldiers," followed by prayers and a reading from the Bible, King spoke to the tense, excited, expectant audience:

My friends, we are certainly very happy to see each of you out this evening. We are here this evening for serious business.

We are here in a general sense because first and foremost, we are American citizens, and we are determined to acquire our citizenship to the fullness of its meaning. We are here also because of our deep-seated belief that democracy transformed from thin paper to thick action is the greatest form of government on earth. But we are here in a specific sense because of the bus situation in Montgomery.

There were so many occasions, he reminded his audience, when Negroes were intimidated and humiliated and oppressed because of the mere fact that they were Negroes. Mrs. Rosa Parks, "one of the finest citizens in Montgomery," had been "taken from a bus and carried to jail and arrested because she refused to give her seat to a white person." But there came a time when people got tired—"tired of being trampled over by the iron feet of oppression . . . tired of being plunged across the abyss of humiliation."

The time had arrived to protest, King insisted. The right to protest was "the great glory of American democracy," and they would protest with unity and grim determination, in the knowledge that the principles of the Constitution and the declarations of the Supreme Court were on their side. They would eschew violence, but also accompany their persuasion with coercion. They would undergird their protest with Christian love, but would also insist upon justice, for love and justice went hand in hand. In closing, King imparted a sense of mission and destiny:

> When the history books are written in the future, somebody will have to say, "There lived a race of people—a *black* people—a people who had the marvellous courage to stand up for their rights, and thereby they injected a new meaning into the veins of history and of civilization." And we are going to do that. God grant that we will do it, before it is too late.

The audience roared their approval.[2]

King had just delivered the kind of oratorical tour de force that would become his hallmark. In simple language couched in the cadences of the black preacher, he had combined emotion, exhortation, and reason in a message of unmistakable clarity. Eschewing complex political arguments, and avoiding any hint of radicalism, he appealed to the basic values of Christianity and American democracy. Striking a skillful balance between militancy and moderation, he aroused righteous anger on the one hand, while stressing discipline and responsibility on the other. He had sensed the mood of the meeting and articulated the unspoken and inchoate feelings of his audience. "This speech had evoked more response than any speech or sermon I had ever delivered," King recalled. "My heart was full. . . . The unity of purpose and *esprit de corps* of these people had been indescribably moving."[3]

But the great test was yet to come. Montgomery's blacks embarked on the boycott confident that the white authorities would soon offer concessions. They were not asking for segregated buses to be abolished, merely that black drivers be employed on mainly black routes, that all drivers treat passengers courteously, and that segregation be truly "separate and equal," with blacks sitting from the rear toward the front and whites seating themselves from the front toward the rear. This "first come, first served" system already operated in several southern cities, including Mobile, Alabama. It obviated the need for blacks to surrender their seats to whites or stand when reserved "white" seats were empty.

In 1955, despite their burning resentment of segregation, blacks in the South felt optimistic that whites would listen to their appeals for fairer treatment with sympathy. After all, the past decade had witnessed unprecedented progress for blacks, with whites accepting a degree of change that would have been unthinkable fifty or even twenty years earlier. Following the Supreme Court's decision in *Smith* v. *Allwright* (1944), which declared that political parties could not legally exclude African Americans from primary elections, the number of registered black voters rose dramatically.

In 1946 about 600,000 black southerners registered, an increase of more than 400,000. By 1952, despite the fact that local white officials controlled the registration process, more than one million blacks had become registered voters. True, this still represented only one black adult in five, and in Deep South states like Alabama and Mississippi the proportion was far smaller. But the overall trend was heartening.

In other spheres, too, blacks had grounds for hope. By the 1950s lynching had virtually ceased: despite the fact that Congress had failed to legislate against the evil, state authorities took steps to stamp it out. In education southern states were finally making an effort to improve provision for blacks by raising the salaries of black teachers, building new schools, and upgrading black colleges. Some southern cities, including Montgomery in 1954, appointed their first black policemen since Reconstruction.

Reinforcing black optimism was a growing belief that the federal government, for so long indifferent to the fate of African Americans, had finally concluded that racial discrimination should no longer enjoy the sanction of law. During World War II blacks had clamored for admission into the armed services only to encounter rigid segregation and pervasive discrimination. In 1950, after years of campaigning by black organizations, President Truman at last ordered segregated military units abolished. Upon becoming President in 1953, Eisenhower supported desegregation within Washington, D.C. And in May 1954 the Supreme Court handed down the pivotal decision *Brown* v. *Board of Education*, which repudiated the "separate but equal" doctrine of *Plessy* v. *Ferguson* and required states with segregated schools to reorganize public education on a "racially nondiscriminatory basis." Blacks did not expect whites to welcome these changes, and they recognized that a degree of legal compulsion would be needed. But the white South had already accommodated to significant change with remarkably good grace.

But when King and other members of the Montgomery Improvement Association (MIA) met with city and bus company officials, they found to their annoyance that the whites adamantly rejected their demands—despite the fact that the company had lost two-thirds of its patronage and that each bus was accumulating a net loss of twenty-two cents a mile. Further negotiating sessions proved equally barren. This unanticipated intransigence on the part of the whites transformed the character of the boycott. At the outset a mild protest designed to win a more polite form of segregation, it evolved into a frontal attack on segregation itself.

Blacks in Montgomery thus became both the victims and beneficiaries of a racial polarization that arose, almost overnight, in the wake of *Brown* v. *Board of Education.* For southern whites, the *Brown* decision represented the last straw. Other changes they had reluctantly swallowed. But they drew the line at allowing their children to attend the same schools as blacks. Working from the deeply ingrained assumption that African Americans were either congenitally or sociologically inferior, they believed that integration would destroy the standards of white schools, corrupt the morals of white children, and bring about the long dreaded "amalgamation" of the races. The prospect of black male teachers instructing white female pupils sent a shudder down the spines of white parents. With a speed and determination that took black people unawares, white southerners organized "massive resistance" to *Brown* and sought to plug every hole that appeared in the wall of segregation. Blacks had to be isolated, their political influence nullified, their legal maneuvers defeated, their protests quashed. The battle lines were drawn.

The black population of Montgomery—fifty thousand men, women, and children—settled in for a long struggle. The day-to-day management of the boycott rested with an executive committee of about forty people, with smaller committees dealing with specialized functions. The subcommittee handling transportation had the most important job, that of keeping the voluntary car pool on the road. It discharged this complex task with impressive efficiency. At a building on the outskirts of Montgomery, the *New York Times* reported, "clerks answered telephones, directed automobiles to passengers . . . and kept the fleet of private cars running smoothly. A battery of bookkeepers and secretaries worked at long tables handling . . . the hundreds of details involved in running a public—and voluntary—transportation system."[4]

But many blacks simply walked. When asked why, one elderly woman replied, "Honey, I have washed and ironed clothes till my legs and body ached. What does it matter now if I still ache, 'cause my mind is now at peace with God." A janitor expressed the same sentiment. "I walk several miles every day up and down this building, so a few more miles for a right cause won't hurt. They know we're right and got the law on our side and that's what they is scared about. The world knows we are right, and we is gonna win our cause. We ain't even worried. White folks don't scare us no longer."[5]

During the first two months of 1956, the Montgomery bus boycott took on the characteristics of a social movement. As blacks shed their initial doubts and fears, they surprised even themselves with their strength. Two experiences had a key influence in forging this unity. In January the city commission embarked on a "get tough" policy designed to break the boycott. The MIA had organized a voluntary car pool that proved a model of efficient transportation: the police began to stop, question, and arrest black drivers; on January 26, they arrested King himself. Four days later, a stick of dynamite exploded outside King's home, blasting the porch and shattering the living-room windows.

Rushing back from a mass meeting, King found an angry black crowd, many of them armed, jeering the mayor, commissioner of public safety, and white policemen. He quickly averted a potential riot by appealing for calm. "Now let's not get panicky. If you

---

have weapons, take them home; if you do not have them, please do not seek to get them. We cannot solve this problem through retaliatory violence. We must meet violence with nonviolence." He assured the onlookers that even if he were killed, the movement would continue. The incident added immeasurably to King's stature. And the "get tough" policy failed to divide or intimidate. On the contrary: on February 1, two days after the bombing, the MIA's lawyer, Fred Gray, filed suit in federal court to challenge the validity of Alabama's bus segregation laws. Blacks in Montgomery had crossed their Rubicon.

Three weeks later, a local grand jury indicted the entire MIA leadership, more than one hundred individuals, for violating a 1921 antiboycott law originally designed to hamper trade unions. The tactic backfired utterly. Instead of fleeing the city to avoid arrest, the leaders boldly presented themselves at the courthouse. E. D. Nixon, a crusty Pullman-car porter who had helped to instigate the boycott, and whose home had been the target of a bomb, was the first to surrender. "You are looking for me?" he asked the startled policemen. "Here I am."

During the next two days, eighty-nine people, including twenty-four ministers, walked into the courthouse to the applause and delight of black onlookers, who had gathered outside the building in a planned show of strength. Smiling and joking as they marched up the steps, their composure flabbergasted the white authorities and thrilled the black community. At a mass meeting on February 24, enthusiasm for the protest had never been higher. Thousands of people filled the church and spilled into the street. White reporters were awed by the emotional atmosphere, groping for words to describe it. "They chanted and sang," wrote one. "They shouted and prayed; they collapsed in the aisles and they sweltered in an eighty-five degree heat. They pledged themselves again and again to 'passive resistance.'" King, delivering the main address, stressed the need for love. "We must have compassion and understanding for those who hate us. We must realize so many people are taught to hate us that they are not totally responsible for their hate." The efforts of white officialdom to pick off the boycott leaders had merely enhanced their prestige among the black rank and file.[6]

The increasing respect accorded the ministers was especially noteworthy, for it confirmed the central role that the black church had assumed in the protest. The boycott had been initiated by laypeople. Jo Ann Robinson, a black college teacher, had been advocating a bus boycott since 1953; she and other members of the Women's Political Council seized on the Rosa Parks incident to put this idea into effect. Together with E. D. Nixon, a former president of the local NAACP, they organized the first day's boycott and only then involved the ministers. They knew, however, that this kind of community-wide protest needed the institutional strength of the black church. Ministers could front the boycott because, unlike most blacks, they were not beholden to white employers. Equally important, the church reached virtually every black family; as a means of mobilization and communication it had no rival. As the boycott unfolded, the churches acted as nodes in the transportation network and provided a means of raising funds. But the church's role soon took on a deeper significance. At first nervous about revealing their identities, the black ministers found hidden reserves of courage as the community closed ranks around them. More than merely supportive and instrumental, the church now defined the character of the movement, infusing it with religious idealism and evangelical fervor. The twice-weekly mass meetings harnessed the emotional strength of black Christianity and stamped the boycott with the kind of moral assurance that was above politics.[7]

For King, too, there was no looking back. His selection as spokesman conferred no particular authority; it did not imply recognition as leader. As one participant put it, "The indignation and demands for action by the 'common people' swept everyone along like a flood." Six weeks into the boycott, white reporters still expressed uncertainty as to who was leading the protest. By the end of February, however, there was no doubt in anybody's mind that King occupied a position of particular eminence. He came to dominate the mass meetings; many regarded him with something like awe. "When King comes in . . . you can hear a pin drop," one observer noted. "He walks in, so calm and quiet, almost like a little boy." When he spoke, the effect was extraordinary. A visitor from Fisk University was struck, in particular, by the adulation he received from women (who often comprised a majority of the mass meetings). Typical remarks were: "He's next to Jesus himself." "We sure are with him." "He's my darling." "He's right there by God." King, for his part, came to realize that blacks wanted and needed a symbol with whom they could identify. Providentially, he had become that symbol, and it was a role he accepted.[8]

At the time of the mass indictments, Daddy King implored his son to retreat to the safety of Atlanta. But the younger King, angry at his father's tactics—he had assembled a group of Atlanta notables, including Benjamin Mays, to put pressure on his son— flatly refused. It would be the height of cowardice to abandon the struggle, he told them. He would rather spend the next ten years in jail than desert the black people of Montgomery. As Daddy King wept, he insisted on going back. It was a poignant and significant moment—King's final declaration of independence from his father, and his conscious acceptance of the leadership that had been thrust upon him almost unawares three months earlier. "As I became involved," he later explained, "and as people began to derive inspiration from their involvement, I realized that the choice leaves your own hands. The people expect you to give them leadership. You see them growing as they move into action, and then you know you no longer have a choice. You can't decide whether to stay in it or get out of it—you must stay in it."[9]

His arrest and conviction turned King into a hero and martyr. "Tonight I stand before you," he told a mass meeting on March 22, "a convicted minister." He continued:

> I seem to have committed three sins. I have done three things that are wrong. First of all, being born a Negro. That is my first sin. Second, being tired of segregation. I have committed the sin of being tired of the injustices and discriminations heaped upon us. Third, having the moral courage to sit up and express our tiredness. That is my third sin.

An audience of three thousand in Holt Street Baptist Church—the first of several mass meetings that evening—gave him "a thunderous burst of applause and cheering." King had learned an invaluable lesson: the more that whites persecuted him, the more that blacks rallied around him and supported the cause he represented. King articulated the movement's aspirations and acted as a lightning rod for the repression of the segregationists.[10]

Yet, fine preacher and brave man that he was, his role entailed more than symbolism. Perhaps the most vital personal quality King brought to his position, in addition to courage and integrity, was that of equanimity. For all his oratorical fireworks in church, away from the pulpit his demeanor was quiet, reserved, almost impassive. In the chaos and turmoil of the moment his self-possession rubbed off on those around him. "Martin was the most imperturbable person I have ever known," one acquaintance recalled. "That inspired a kind of calmness when you would expect that all hell was going to break loose." This outward self-assurance, including a determination not to be provoked, helped the movement to resist rash decisions in moments of great pressure. After the bombing of his home, noted one observer, King "never showed any signs of breaking." His coolness, his refusal to panic, helped him to defuse crises. An easygoing manner enabled him to get along with people and mediate personal disputes.[11]

King was not a particularly good negotiator. Accustomed to academic discussion, he lacked the kind of debating skills—the ability to score points and split hairs—necessary to pin down quick-witted opponents. He did not possess the shallow nimble-mindedness of the lawyer or politician. King's intellectual depth and his experience in dealing with white people, made him adept, however, at interpreting the boycott to the outside world. By the early months of 1956, reporters from local, regional, national, and even foreign newspapers were knocking at his door. Articulate and accessible, King provided them with instant copy. Journalists were fascinated by his grasp of philosophy and found his speeches immensely quotable.

Caught up in a protest that devoured his time and energy, King had thus far given little thought to the wider significance of the boycott or to his own future. In the North, however, left-wing activists hailed the protest as a historical turning point. For two decades and more, the Communist Party, the Socialist Party, the Congress of Industrial Organizations (CIO) and other radical groups had been trying to crack the South's racial caste system. Although the CIO unions had made some limited gains in organizing black and white workers, the wall of segregation remained intact. Without mass support from inside the South, the efforts of northern-based organizations to reform the South collapsed under the weight of racism and state repression.

If prejudice kept white and black workers apart, then blacks would have to organize their own resistance to Jim Crow. As far back as the 1920s, some opponents of racism pointed to the example of Gandhi and his campaigns of nonviolent resistance against British rule in India. In 1932 Reinhold Niebuhr, as we have seen, argued that blacks in the South would be able to utilize

nonviolent tactics to good effect. Ten years later a group of pacifists organized the Congress of Racial Equality (CORE) for the
specific purpose of encouraging nonviolent direct action against
racial discrimination. And in 1943 the African-American leader
A. Philip Randolph, president of the Brotherhood of Sleeping
Car Porters, an all-black labor union, proposed that blacks in
the South oppose Jim Crow by conducting one-day boycotts of
segregated schools, railroads, streetcars, and buses.

But plans for Gandhi-style campaigns of mass civil disobedience remained on the level of theory. CORE's protests were confined to the North, and they involved very few people. Randolph's
proposals for mass boycotts elicited no practical response in the
South. In the 1940s, blacks were not yet ready for a direct assault upon segregation; it seemed more important to concentrate
on obtaining the vote and tackling more immediate problems of
want and neglect. Above all, fear of white violence inhibited the
adoption of Gandhian tactics. Open defiance of the white authorities, blacks believed, would lead to serious bloodshed and gain
nothing.

The few attempts to practice nonviolent direct action in the
South before 1955 had not inspired confidence in the technique.
In 1947 members of CORE and the Fellowship of Reconciliation (FOR), a pacifist group, challenged bus segregation by sitting together as they rode through Maryland, Virginia, West Virginia, and North Carolina. The eight blacks and eight whites
were harassed, intimidated, and arrested; three of them served
brief sentences on a North Carolina chain gang. This "Journey of
Reconciliation" signally failed to arouse mass support, and buses
remained segregated. In 1948 Henry Wallace, running for President as head of the Progressive Party, insisted that all his campaign meetings should be integrated and refused to avail himself
of segregated hotels and restaurants. Predictably, white thugs and
hecklers made a shambles of Wallace's rallies. In Birmingham,

Alabama, police commissioner "Bull" Connor banned nonsegre-
gated meetings and arrested Senator Glen Taylor, Wallace's running mate. Direct action seemed hopeless against this type of
repression. The NAACP advised blacks travelling on trains and
buses to obey the segregation laws lest they incite the "violent
proclivities" of white officials.

Pacifists devoted to Gandhian tactics—groups like CORE and
the FOR—were quick to grasp the significance of the Montgomery bus boycott, and they immediately speculated on the possibility of spreading its example throughout the South. But they
also feared that without the right kind of guidance and discipline,
the Montgomery movement might succumb to white provocation
and disintegrate, causing a great historical opportunity to be lost.
The leaders needed a thorough grounding in the philosophy and
techniques of nonviolence, they believed.

Such considerations prompted Bayard Rustin, an associate of
A. Philip Randolph, founder of CORE, and veteran of the "Journey of Reconciliation," to visit Montgomery in order to assess the
movement there. He found King responsive to his ideas: he was
interested in Gandhi, but admitted to only a superficial understanding of nonviolence. King welcomed Rustin's help—the new
emphasis on "passive resistance" that appeared in his speeches
reflected Rustin's influence. Another pacifist, Glenn Smiley, also
urged King to study and accept nonviolence. A white southerner,
and an ordained minister in the Methodist church, Smiley worked
for the Fellowship of Reconciliation. King hugely impressed him
on their first meeting: "I believe that God has called Martin
Luther King to lead a great movement here and in the South," he
reported. He added:

> [He] wants to do it right, but is too young and some of his
> close help is violent. King accepts . . . a body guard, and asked
> for a permit for them to carry guns. This was denied by the

police, but nevertheless, the place is an arsenal. King sees the inconsistency but not enough. He believes and yet he doesn't believe. . . . If he can *really* be won to a faith in non-violence there is no end to what he can do.

King could become either a "Negro Gandhi," Smiley predicted, or "an unfortunate demagogue destined to swing from a lynch mob's tree." After much debate and soul-searching, King decided to adopt nonviolence as an unshakeable principle. He forbade his drivers and bodyguards to carry firearms, and he gave no further thought to acquiring a gun himself.

By April 1956 the Montgomery bus boycott showed no signs of ending. The Chicago-based company that operated the buses was prepared to abandon segregation, but the three-man Montgomery city council refused to permit this. The MIA, moreover, had moved beyond its original demand for a more equitable form of segregation. "The protest will no longer settle for this," Glenn Smiley noted, "for they are really generating power by these mass meetings." The governor of Alabama, James Folsom, privately sympathized with the blacks, but his attempts to mediate the dispute failed.[12]

The federal judiciary finally broke the deadlock. On June 5 a panel of three judges—white southerners all—ruled that Alabama's bus segregation law discriminated against blacks and was hence unconstitutional. It was a major landmark, because in extending the reasoning of *Brown* v. *Board of Education* it implied that the federal courts would eventually invalidate all state and local laws that mandated segregation in public facilities. Despite a dissent by one of the judges and the prospect of a lengthy appeal by the Montgomery city council, *Browder* v. *Gayle* buoyed the protesters and brought victory within sight. The boycott continued into the summer and autumn, brimming with confidence. "The people are just as enthusiastic now as they were in the beginning of the protest," King marvelled. "They are determined never to return to Jim Crow buses. The mass meetings are still jammed and packed and above all the buses are still empty." [13]

On November 13 the U.S. Supreme Court affirmed that bus segregation was unconstitutional. Further appeals and legal maneuvers delayed implementation of the order, but the city finally bowed to the inevitable. On December 21, 1956—the first day of integration—King boarded a bus and took a seat near the front. A white man, Glenn Smiley, sat next to him. This simple act marked a historic victory for black southerners: the beginning of the end of racial segregation. The Montgomery bus boycott had been a massive collective effort, but King had done more than anyone else to hold it together and give it moral resonance. For a young man of twenty-seven, it was a remarkable achievement.

3

Prophet of Nonviolence

On January 10, 1957, less than two months after blacks in Montgomery returned to integrated buses, King convened a meeting of about sixty black leaders, mostly ministers, at his father's church in Atlanta. Out of this gathering emerged a new organization that, after several name changes, called itself the Southern Christian Leadership Conference (SCLC). King was elected president, a position he held until his assassination. The aim of SCLC was to build upon the success of the Montgomery bus boycott; for the next eleven years it became the vehicle through which King mobilized black southerners to protest against segregation and discrimination. SCLC's motto, "To Redeem the Soul of America," reflected both its Christian orientation and its commitment to nonviolence.

On the surface, nonviolence seemed consonant with King's religious beliefs and appeared to develop logically from the emphasis upon Christian love that appeared in his very first speech as spokesman for the bus boycott. Some have even argued that certain character traits that had been evident as far back as early childhood—an "abhorrence of violence" and a "desire to assume the suffering of others"—predisposed him to the self-sacrificing nature of nonviolence.[1] Yet King's was not an overnight conversion. As a youth he had been no stranger to fisticuffs; as a student his reading of Niebuhr had made him skeptical about pacifism; as an African American in the Deep South, he had no illusions about the readiness of whites to employ violence. King's commitment to nonviolence was a major turning point in his life.

Nonviolence could be defined narrowly or widely. In the first instance, it simply denoted abstention from violence, for pragmatic or other reasons. It could also define a method of protest, mass nonviolent direct action, sometimes called passive or nonviolent resistance. In the broadest sense of the term, as a philosophical commitment, nonviolence aspired to bring about reconciliation among classes, races, and nations. By protesting in a *spirit* of nonviolence, King insisted, and by demonstrating a willingness to suffer without striking back, blacks would defeat racism while at the same time educating whites in the error of their ways and paving the way for interracial amity. Through the power of love, blacks would win the hearts and consciences of their oppressors. Nonviolence was the path to a "Beloved Community," the actualization of the "Kingdom of God," a society "in which men and women live as children of God should live . . . a kingdom controlled by the law of love."[2]

The United States seemed unpromising soil upon which to cast these seeds. It possessed no tradition of nonviolence and placed little value on self-sacrifice. In a land that defined the possession of arms as a fundamental right, a society that esteemed political power, commercial cunning, and legal sleight of hand, it seemed bizarre to suggest that any group—least of all blacks—could get anywhere by impressing its adversaries with its capacity to suffer. Over the years critics would attack King's stance as naïve, demeaning, ineffective, and even pathological. During the boycott, blacks in Montgomery were bemused and often skeptical about it, seeing no need to accompany their direct action with professions of love for the very whites who were harassing, prosecuting, and bombing them.

For King, however, philosophy and practice went hand in hand. The possibility that some blacks, goaded beyond endurance by Klan bombings and continual provocation by the white authorities, might resort to arms had posed an ever-present threat to the success of the bus boycott. Although any recourse to violence on the part of the black minority seemed suicidal, many ordinary people admitted they would retaliate against white aggression with alacrity. "These white folks keep messing up," a black maid stated forcefully. "They gonna have a war if they keep going. We just be forced to kill 'em all cause if they hurt Reverend King I don't mind dying, but I sure am taking a white bastard with me. If I don't have my razor with me, I'll use a stick." A member of his own congregation took King aside one day and suggested "killing off" a number of whites. "This is the only language these white folks will understand," he told the appalled pastor. Many others, like E. D. Nixon, refused to abjure self-defense. "There isn't any use in your telling me that if a man slaps me, I'm not to slap him back," he told King. "I know that before I could think about what you said, I'm going to have knocked the guy's block off."[3]

King knew, however, that a single instance of black violence might cause the disintegration of the boycott. He needed to convince blacks of the futility of aggressive violence; but he also— a much more difficult task—had to persuade them that violence in self-defense could be equally disastrous. The line between aggression and defense would be impossible to maintain: it would be simple for the police to provoke an incident in order to supply the white authorities with an excuse to employ massive force. Unity required discipline, and discipline demanded a refusal to be provoked. Nonviolence thus fulfilled a practical function that all could be made to understand. It also performed the difficult task of maintaining a level of determined but controlled militancy.

By distinguishing between the evil and the evildoer, by stressing the necessity for reconciliation, and by curbing inflammatory language, nonviolence helped to restrain the kind of antiwhite feelings that, left unchecked, might lead to impulsive acts of individual violence.

When King spoke of "nonviolence" he tended to conflate the various meanings of the term, employing, one suspects, deliberate ambiguity. By making a virtue of necessity—any resort to violence on the part of blacks would be suicidal—he reinforced the claim of black southerners to represent a superior morality to that of the white racists. By emphasizing "love" rather than pressure—even to the extent of dropping the term "boycott"—he distinguished the methods of the boycotters from the kind of economic coercion that the segregationist Citizens Councils directed against blacks who attempted to vote or send their children to white schools.

While the great majority of blacks had difficulty accepting nonviolence as a philosophy, the success of the boycott testified to its efficacy as a technique. Nonviolence not only promoted unity and discipline among the blacks but also inhibited the employment of violence by the whites. Indeed, the relative *lack* of white violence represented one of the most remarkable aspects of the Montgomery story. Before the boycott, fear of white violence had rendered mass direct action a nonstarter. As the bus protest unfolded, however, the white authorities were restrained in their use of violence by the ostentatious nonviolence of their opponents and by the worldwide publicity accorded the protest after the January bombings. The Montgomery bus boycott set a pattern for many subsequent civil rights struggles: whites would generally use "legal" means, rather than violence, in their efforts to suppress black protests. This was a significant victory in itself.

Nonviolence also dispelled, or at least mitigated, the black fear of white officialdom and terror of southern jails. It helped blacks take everything that was thrown at them—the ban on taxis giving free lifts, the bombing of homes and churches, the indictment of the leaders, the conviction of King for organizing the boycott, the harassment of drivers, the cancellation of car insurance policies, the court injunction against the motor pool—and carry on regardless. For blacks, the Montgomery bus boycott represented a psychological breakthrough. "We just ain't scared of these people no longer," affirmed one woman, "and we gonna let 'em know so through 'Peace' and 'Love.'" Glenn Smiley was amazed by the irony of the situation: "[W]hites are scared stiff and Negroes are calm as cucumbers." As Bayard Rustin put it, the movement gave blacks "the feeling that they could be bigger and stronger and more courageous and more loving than they thought they could be."[4]

SCLC tried to capitalize on this new fearlessness. But the people who designed the new organization recognized that nonviolence also had, at least potentially, a radical political edge. Indeed, SCLC might not have come into being but for the political foresight of three northern radicals: Bayard Rustin, Stanley David Levison, and Ella Jo Baker. Levison, a Jew, was a wealthy New Yorker who, although trained as a lawyer, had made most of his money by shrewd investments in various small businesses. Baker, an African-American woman, was a native of North Carolina who had moved to New York in 1927 and resided there ever since.

These three New Yorkers shared radical political convictions, a passionate hatred of racism, and extensive organizational experience. A generation older than King, they had reached political maturity in the late 1930s and 1940s, when New York was a maelstrom of left-wing activism, and when the Communist Party to a large extent set the pace in the field of civil rights. Young radicals like Rustin, Levison, and Baker admired the Communists for their flamboyant techniques of mass agitation and willingness to practice what they preached when it came to racial equality. Rustin was briefly a member of the Young Communist League, and Levison may have joined the Communist Party itself. Such flirtations with Communism were neither shocking nor surprising. This was, after all, a period of "popular fronts," when Communists, Socialists, trade unionists, churchmen, and liberals of every stripe regularly cooperated.

By the mid-1950s, however, American radicalism had withered under the impact of the Cold War and the blight of McCarthyism. The enunciation of the Truman Doctrine in 1947 signalled an end to cooperation with the Soviet Union and rendered the maintenance of popular fronts, even on domestic issues, impossible. The Truman administration, convinced that it had to "scare hell out of the American people" in order to win popular support for rearmament and the "containment" of Soviet influence, depicted American Communists as a threat to national security. In 1949 the government prosecuted the leaders of the Communist Party for allegedly advocating and planning a violent revolution; they were convicted and jailed. Shortly afterward, Senator Joseph McCarthy embarked on an obsessive hunt for real and supposed Communists in a hysterical binge that, aided by passions unleashed by the Korean War, lasted four years. Although McCarthy lost his personal influence in 1954 and died three years later, all forms of left-wing radicalism remained deeply suspect. By the end of 1956, after the Soviet Union's suppression of the Hungarian uprising, the Communist Party was isolated, discredited, persecuted, drastically reduced in numbers, and riddled with FBI informers.

As important as the fate of the Party itself was the demise of satellite organizations it dominated or influenced. The Southern Negro Youth Congress expired in 1948 and the Civil Rights Congress—both tarred as Communist "fronts"—died in 1956. The CIO expelled eleven ostensibly Communist-led trade unions in 1949–50, sending them into rapid decline. Even liberal organizations fell victim to the virus of intolerance: the Southern Conference for Human Welfare, an interracial group that had been founded in 1938 with the encouragement of President Roosevelt himself, dissolved ten years later after persistent attacks for alleged Communism. Its successor, the Southern Conference Education Fund, was hounded by state and congressional committees well into the 1960s.

The destruction of the "Old Left," with its commitment to mass action and labor solidarity, removed one of the biggest potential threats to the racial caste system. Rustin, Levison, and Baker believed that the absence of mass pressure had brought the fight against segregation and discrimination to a virtual standstill. But they and other left-wing activists had nowhere to go. The NAACP now virtually monopolized the civil rights field but had become increasingly conservative in its methods and outlook. Under the leadership of Walter White and his successor, Roy Wilkins, the NAACP concentrated almost exclusively on lobbying Congress and instituting test cases in the federal courts. Although it had a paid-up membership approaching half a million, it disdained the techniques of mass agitation—demonstrations, boycotts, emotional propaganda, provocative gestures—favored by the left. In the eyes of its critics, the organization had ossified into a top-heavy bureaucracy and was increasingly ineffective.

The NAACP, of course, stoutly defended its methods. It could point to its success in winning important court cases, notably *Brown* v. *Board of Education*. It could even claim that the desegregation of Montgomery's buses vindicated its strategy of challenging segregation in the courts. Some historians have agreed with this assessment, pointing out that the MIA's victory was secured by litigation, which the NAACP helped to finance and argue, rather than the boycott itself. Moreover, without the assistance of the federal courts the boycott would have collapsed, for in November the city council obtained an injunction against the car pool, thus bringing the MIA's transportation system to a standstill.[5]

But this is too narrow an interpretation. To assume that social change flows from litigation is to abstract the legal process from political reality. In theory, virtually any individual or group could institute a lawsuit against some aspect of segregation; in theory, the federal courts would rule that segregation violated the Fourteenth Amendment; in theory, when a court so ruled, southern whites accepted the result. In practice, however, the NAACP's litigation strategy worked nothing like this and proved far less effective than anticipated.

The NAACP experienced the utmost difficulty in persuading individual blacks to act as plaintiffs; in the extreme case of Mississippi, it could not file a single school desegregation suit. Federal judges, moreover, did not always rule in the NAACP's favor. Some were convinced segregationists who exhibited blatant bias. Others felt intimidated by the strength of white feeling against integration, fearing social ostracism if they furthered it. Many judges— including those of the Supreme Court—leaned over backward to appear reasonable to the southern whites, allowing them delay after delay. But few southern whites were disposed to accept the integrationist edicts of the Supreme Court, as their reaction to *Brown* v. *Board of Education* graphically illustrated. Throughout the South, political leadership passed into the hands of men who advocated outright defiance of *Brown* or, at best, token compliance. Finally, in the absence of strong legislation by Congress, each city and county had to be treated as a separate entity, requiring the NAACP to fight dozens, and eventually hundreds, of simultaneous legal battles. This courtroom war overwhelmed the NAACP.

By 1956 the white campaign of "massive resistance" to school desegregation had already taken form. Yet while segregationist leaders mobilized popular support for their obstructionist tactics, the NAACP continued to rely almost exclusively upon the courts. Moreover, many blacks were unenthusiastic about school desegregation, for it threatened the jobs of black teachers and endangered institutions that were cornerstones of community life. In the absence of mass support, black plaintiffs were painfully isolated, becoming exposed targets for white intimidation.

In the case of the Montgomery bus boycott, mass direct action had generated *effective* litigation. The successful suit originated in the boycott, and the urgency of the crisis speeded up the judicial process, making for an early, favorable decision by the federal courts. It is possible, of course, that blacks in Montgomery would have challenged the bus segregation law anyway, even if the boycott had never taken place. But it stretches credulity to believe that mere coincidence ordained that the first successful suit against bus segregation should arise from the first sustained bus boycott. Mass direct action generated the kind of pressure that compelled the federal courts to respond—in cities where blacks relied upon litigation alone, it often took years to desegregate buses.

Mass direct action also gave blacks the confidence to assert their newly-won rights. In many southern towns—including Baton Rouge, where the leaders had called off the boycott prematurely—bus segregation lingered on into the early 1960s because blacks feared to challenge custom even when it no longer had the force of law. There was no such hesitancy in Montgomery. As Glenn Smiley put it, the major obstacle to desegregation was "a willingness to accept discrimination and low morale" on the part of blacks. Only nonviolent mass action created "a sense of oneness, of movement, and of resistance," causing black southerners "to move into the land and possess it."[6]

Rustin, Levison, and Baker contended that without this kind of mass action, progress in dismantling white supremacy would be stymied by the political deadlock that all but paralyzed the federal government. In 1948 the Truman administration had finally endorsed a series of measures designed to guarantee black civil rights. But the southern Democrats killed Truman's program through use of their veto power in the Senate. In the mid-1950s the Democratic Party remained deeply divided on the issue; even in concert with sympathetic Republicans, northern liberal Democrats had been unable to enact a single civil rights measure of any significance. Congress took no steps to enforce *Brown,* and President Eisenhower even refused to endorse the decision, with which he privately disagreed. As far as civil rights was concerned, the federal government resembled a three-engine plane limping along on a single engine—the judiciary—and even that engine showed signs of stopping.

In stressing the importance of mass action, King's advisers harkened back to the 1930s, when black and white workers had made giant strides forward under the banner of the CIO. The labor movement of that period, wrote Levison, "used the weapon of the strike, boycotts, marches and varied demonstrations. . . . The sacrifices of striking workers, the hunger they endured, the blood they spilled from their own bodies, the involvement of their wives and children . . . finally won for them their established place." Black people in the South were ready to make a similar commitment, but they had to be inspired, organized, and led. To Roy Wilkins, who dismissed demonstrations as a way of "blowing off steam," Levison replied, "They do that too, but the steam propels a piston which drives the train forward."[7]

King readily agreed that mass pressure from southern blacks themselves would be needed to break this impasse. If the example of Montgomery could be duplicated throughout the South, a local victory could be translated into a strategic breakthrough. In discussions with Bayard Rustin, as well as in several meetings organized by Smiley and the Fellowship of Reconciliation, King moved toward the idea of establishing a new organization in the South, based on the black church, that would promote nonviolence. The precipitous decline of the NAACP gave the idea added impetus. In 1956 state authorities embarked on a campaign of legal harassment intended to destroy the NAACP's southern presence. In Alabama a state court forced the NAACP to disband completely; the organization survived in other states, but with a fraction of its former membership. The successful conclusion of the Montgomery bus boycott provided an obvious opportunity for launching a new organization. Blacks in Montgomery had not only won desegregation of the buses, but they had also won the propaganda war hands down. Their cause had evoked worldwide sympathy, thrown an international spotlight on the Deep South, and prompted an influx of financial support from around the globe. Having seized the initiative in such a spectacular fashion, it was imperative for blacks to retain it.

SCLC's structure and program were dictated partly by circumstance and partly by the strategic vision of King, Rustin, Levison, and Baker. In light of the MIA's success, it made obvious sense to base the organization on the black church. As Rustin put it, the church represented "the most stable institution of the southern Negro community." The church had given the Montgomery bus boycott unity, coherence, and an extraordinary crusading quality that came to be known as the "movement spirit." Above all, the church facilitated mass participation. Ironically, the formal democracy of the NAACP militated against mass involvement, while the informal autocracy of the black church encouraged it. The NAACP held regular branch meetings, open to paid-up members, and conducted according to the rule book. The MIA's mass meetings were open to all, offering a carefully orchestrated program of hymns, prayers, and inspirational speeches. The MIA had been a "movement" rather than an organization. SCLC hoped to emulate that movement on a wider basis.

There were also sound tactical reasons for structuring SCLC around the black church. Churches had the advantage of being relatively invulnerable to persecution. They were independent institutions that blacks themselves owned and controlled. Un-

like corporations—a legal category into which the NAACP fell—
they were free from government regulation. Moreover, the black
church enjoyed a degree of respect from white southerners, and
officials in the South—often called the Bible Belt—would think
twice before harrying ministers. Similar considerations accounted
for SCLC's lack of individual members. The NAACP had been
compelled to furnish its membership lists to state officials; the
lists had then been publicized and the members subjected to intimidation and reprisals. SCLC's access to black churches gave it
a potential "membership" of millions, but the absence of membership lists made it difficult for white officials to single out individuals.

There is a certain irony in the fact that SCLC, an organization dedicated to integration, made no attempt formally to involve whites. Whites could support SCLC morally, politically, and
financially, but they did not acquire any official voice in its delib-
erations.

In part, SCLC's all-black composition simply reflected political realities in the South, where the strength of racism ruled out
black-white coalitions. But the exclusion of whites was also deliberate. Bayard Rustin's experience convinced him that interracial
organizations had two serious drawbacks. The first was that of
Communist entryism. Having seen the Communist Party ma-
nipulate other organizations for its own sectarian ends, and sensitive to the conservative climate of the 1950s, he hoped to insulate
SCLC from possible Communist influence. Rustin also believed
that the presence of whites militated against black involvement
because blacks tended to be awed by whites, especially articulate intellectuals. The history of CORE, the interracial group that
Rustin helped found in 1942, illustrated this point. CORE had
never attracted mass support and in 1956 seemed moribund. In
structuring SCLC Rustin looked back to the all-black March
on Washington movement, the campaign against job discrimina-

tion in the defense industries organized by A. Philip Randolph, Rustin's mentor, in 1941. He also drew an obvious lesson from the Montgomery bus boycott. Blacks took great pride in the fact that they themselves organized, led, and to a large extent financed the boycott; it had been their own movement.

King knew very well that the problem of racism was national in scope. He also recognized that by adopting an exclusively southern orientation, SCLC would be able to maximize support from northern whites. Moreover, although they all suffered from racial discrimination, blacks in the North and blacks in the South faced different obstacles that required different strategies. Unlike those in the North, blacks in the South were oppressed by a racial caste system that had the force of law. This system had functioned as a means of securing an abundant supply of cheap, subservient black labor for southern plantation agriculture. As the South evolved, however, from an almost feudal system into a more fully developed capitalism, the barriers of caste were becoming increasingly wasteful. Rustin and Levison believed that big business would itself support the removal of those barriers, if only out of economic self-interest. The problems of blacks in the North derived from the nature of capitalism itself, but in the South, capitalism was the unwitting ally of African Americans. Sound strategy required that the two struggles should be kept separate. In this way southern blacks could enlist the support of northern liberals, and even conservatives.

Although King readily comprehended them, such arguments mattered little to most of the black ministers who made up SCLC. For them, the decision to confine the organization to the South was a shrewdly practical one. Southern whites never tired of repeating that "their" blacks were basically content, and that the races would live in harmony were it not for "outside agitators" who "stirred up trouble." Communists rated top billing in the segregationist demonology and the NAACP came a close second.

The NAACP's headquarters were in New York, a fact that lent superficial credence to the charge that its integrationist policies commanded little support among blacks in the South. The Montgomery bus boycott gave the lie to this charge because it was entirely local in origin, composition, and leadership. Indeed, in forming an independent organization instead of working through the NAACP, the boycott leaders betrayed their sensitivity to the charge of outside manipulation. In the same way, SCLC could claim to speak for southern blacks because it was indigenous to the South.

The need to project independent black leadership in the South also dictated that Rustin, Levison, and Baker stay very much in the background—so much so that their behind-the-scenes work assisting King went largely unnoticed. The role of the three New Yorkers should not be exaggerated, however. The basic impetus of the civil rights movement, mass nonviolent direct action, came from the South. SCLC was a logical extension of the Montgomery bus boycott: that protest had such a profound impact that it generated many different proposals for the formation of a wider organization. In addition, the suppression of the NAACP in Alabama created a leadership vacuum that cried out to be filled. Without King himself, however, SCLC might never have taken shape. Indeed, it would be difficult to overstate the prestige and authority that accrued to him from his leadership of the Montgomery bus boycott. Perhaps it would have succeeded without him; we shall never know. At the time, his contribution seemed indispensable. As Levison put it many years later, "[F]orty-eight thousand black people . . . were almost 100 per cent united in Montgomery. That was new. That, nobody had ever done before." King's task now was to repeat that miracle across the South.[8]

4

In Search of a Movement

IF KING FELT ELATED by his sudden fame, he also experienced fear, bewilderment, frustration, and exhaustion. After December 5, 1955, the responsibilities of leadership extended his days, squeezed his nights, ate into his pastoral duties, and crowded his family life. Seven months into the Montgomery bus boycott, his doctor told him to ease his workload, but the pressure of the situation permitted no letup. "I still find myself so involved I hardly have time to breathe," he reported to Rustin. The end of the boycott brought little respite: the presidency of SCLC entailed never-ending correspondence, publishers' deadlines, constant travel, and speeches without end. In the midst of doing so many things, King complained, "I am not doing anything well." He found "the general strain of being known" disorienting. And he feared that his inability to study and reflect was making him intellectually stale. "My whole life seems to be centered around giving something out and only rarely taking something in," he told one of his former theology professors. "I know that I cannot continue to go at this pace, and live with such a tension filled schedule."[1]

Yet something impelled him to carry on at the same hectic pace.

Unkind critics suggested that success had gone to his head or that base material motives drove him. Others offered deeper explanations. Ella Baker speculated that King shared the competitiveness of Atlanta's black middle class, viewing public fame as another feather in the King family's cap. Stanley Levison, however, believed that the tributes King received strengthened his determination to serve the underprivileged. "Martin could be described as an intensely guilt-ridden man," he thought. "If he had been less humble, he could have lived with this great acclaim; but as it was, he always thought of ways in which he could somehow live up to it." According to Bayard Rustin, King was "always struggling to make sure that he was trying to do the right thing in the right way," a process accompanied by considerable inner turmoil.[2]

With his motives under question, King responded with increased commitment and deeper religious faith. Biographer David J. Garrow suggests that a religious experience one January night in 1956 transformed King's life. Tired and afraid, a threatening telephone call brought him to an emotional and psychological crisis. As King described the incident, when he reached the point of breaking down and deciding to abandon the leadership of the bus boycott, he prayed aloud with his head bowed over the kitchen table. "At that moment I experienced the presence of the Divine as I had never experienced Him before." An inner voice seemed to urge him on, and King returned to the fray with his faith and courage renewed. Whenever King became discouraged, his memory of that moment gave him fresh strength and resolve.[3]

On one occasion, however, King did appear to break down. At a mass meeting shortly after the boycott ended, he felt gripped by an uncontrollable emotion. "Lord, I hope that no one will have to die as a result of our struggle for freedom in Montgomery," he exclaimed. "Certainly, I don't want to die. But if anyone has to die, let it be me." As some members of the audience sobbed and others shouted "No, no," King gripped the pulpit and remained rooted to the spot, speechless. Fellow ministers went to his aid, but it was several minutes before King sat down.[4]

It would be dangerous to take such public expressions of emotion at face value; a cynic might even regard them as the kind of dramatic ploy beloved of preachers. King himself became a past master at manipulating audiences; although he professed to despise the ranting, or "whooping," of uneducated black clergymen, he knew all the tricks of his trade. And he soon learned that references to his own suffering and affirmations of his willingness to die not only aroused intense emotion but also deflected criticism and reinforced unity. His highly public breakdown might also have been caused, at least in part, by a combination of fatigue and stress. Placid and reserved in private, the pulpit King could normally turn emotion on and off like a tap. Over the years, however, extreme physical exhaustion sometimes induced a depression so intense as virtually to immobilize him.

King's religious faith undoubtedly deepened as a result of the boycott. Narrowly surviving the knife-stab of a demented woman during a book-signing ceremony in 1958 also strengthened his conviction that God had singled him out for a particular role. Recuperating from his wound, he had a rare opportunity for contemplation and reflection. As exemplified by Christ's own sacrifice, King believed, his unearned suffering was redemptive. "We felt that we were being prepared for a much larger work," Coretta King remembered, "that, in order to be able to endure the persecution and the suffering ahead, we would have to rededicate ourselves to nonviolence."[5]

King, who was not an ascetic, had come to terms with the moral discipline of the Baptist church by treating its restrictions on personal behavior as minor hypocrisies. Baptist ministers were not supposed to drink or smoke; King privately indulged in both. Money, however, did not interest him, and a visit to India in 1959 to acquaint himself with the legacy of Gandhi reinforced his disdain for material wealth. The bulk of his speaking fees and book royalties went to SCLC; his pastor's salary constituted virtually all of his income. Although he and his family lived comfortably, they enjoyed a modest standard of living by the yardstick of middleclass America. In 1960 King drove a 1954 Pontiac and lived in a small rented house. So important did he regard financial probity that an attempt by the state of Alabama to convict him for tax evasion caused King more distress than practically any other ordeal. The resulting trial vindicated him completely, but baseless rumors of padded expense accounts and money in Swiss banks persisted.

Between SCLC's foundation in 1957 and its demonstrations in Birmingham, Alabama, in 1963, King became the inspirational symbol of the emerging civil rights movement. He established himself as the foremost spokesperson of African Americans in the South. He also developed an acute sensitivity to the mood of ordinary blacks, learning to judge what sacrifices they were prepared to make and, conversely, which tactics demanded too much of them. By 1963, through painful trial and error, he had mastered the art of bending the political system through nonviolent protest.

These were also years of frustration and uncertainty. SCLC's founders hoped that the Montgomery bus boycott would set the South ablaze with mass nonviolent protests, but they were quickly disappointed. Although blacks in Tallahassee, Florida, commenced a bus boycott in May 1956, a wave of bus boycotts did not spontaneously sweep across the South. In many cities, the white authorities recognized the inevitability of change and quietly permitted desegregation. Other cities continued to enforce segregation, and blacks acquiesced in the situation while their legal challenges wound their way through the courts. Black southerners flocked to hear King, but they seemed reluctant to implement his ideas.

The limitations of nonviolence and the circumscribed nature of King's position soon became apparent. The example of Montgomery showed that a mass nonviolent movement could not be sustained indefinitely; a community became exhausted. Once the crisis passed, moreover, the pressure for unity ended: the querulous factionalism of old resurfaced, and King proved unable to build on the MIA's success. As an outsider, a neutral figure, he had helped to unite blacks during the boycott. But now he was part of the landscape, an established leader, the object of jealous looks and critical remarks. Colleagues resented his fame; they muttered about his growing remoteness and authoritarian manner.

King also had to contend with the hostility of the NAACP, which eyed all other civil rights groups with suspicion verging on hostility. It regarded SCLC as a particular threat to its southern operations, and the NAACP's leaders lost no opportunity to belittle the new organization. They planted critical stories in the press, openly disparaged King's ideas about nonviolence, and forbade local NAACP officials to work with SCLC. These petty-minded attempts to undermine him angered King, but he refused to respond in kind: "The job ahead is too great . . . to be bickering in the darkness of jealousy, deadening competition, and internal ego struggles."[6]

The conservatism of the African-American church also hampered King. Although SCLC based itself on the church, there was a world of difference between assembling a small group of activists and welding the black church into a coherent political force. Many black ministers regarded nonviolent direct action as dangerously radical and wanted nothing to do with the civil rights movement. Joseph H. Jackson, the president of the National Baptist Convention—the world's largest organization of black Baptists—openly disparaged King's ideas; other prominent Baptists, such as Abraham Lincoln Davis of New Orleans and Theodore J. Jemison of Baton Rouge, dropped out of SCLC. King hoped to win the Baptist convention's backing for SCLC by ousting Jackson and replacing him with Gardner C. Taylor, a friend and ally. At a decisive meeting in 1961, however, Jackson quashed the Taylor-King challenge. He became one of King's most vociferous black critics.

With or without the National Baptist Convention's backing, the amorphous nature of the Baptist denomination, which accounted for two-thirds of the country's black Christians, rendered the church extremely difficult to mobilize. With each congregation a sovereign body, Baptists were a refractory lot, notoriously reluctant to follow outside authority. At the same time, the absence of an ecclesiastical hierarchy left individual Baptist churches with a good deal of freedom. Thus, through a continuous effort of persuasion and personal contact, King recruited individual ministers to his cause. Without compelling community pressure, however, the majority of black ministers stayed aloof from the civil rights struggle, and King became bitingly critical of their passivity and greed.

King might have given himself entirely to the task of building a mass movement in the South, despite lack of staff and funds. The need to attract support from northern whites, however, dictated that he spend much of his time fund-raising in the North, speaking to northern audiences, and writing books and articles for northern readers. Guided by Rustin and Levison, he also engaged in a good deal of maneuvering to project himself onto the national stage.

At the close of the 1950s King presented a paradox. On the one hand, his efforts to promote nonviolent direct action appeared unsuccessful. Indeed, no sooner had SCLC been formed than it switched its focus to voter registration. This was partly an opportunistic response to the 1957 Civil Rights Act, a bipartisan measure that, although mild, rekindled federal interest in the scandal of black disfranchisement. The switch also stemmed from a simple recognition that the example of Montgomery had not been emulated. Even in the field of voter registration, however, King admitted in 1959 that "we have not really scratched the surface." In 1960 he moved to Atlanta to copastor Ebenezer Baptist Church and devote more of his time to SCLC. But the organization made little progress on any front. "Frankly," one colleague complained, "many thoughtful persons are wondering why it is taking us so long to build a mass movement in the South." Ella Baker, who had become SCLC's first staff member, blamed King for this poor showing; she soon left the organization, convinced that a stultifying personality cult was stifling the emergence of a grass-roots movement.[7]

On the other hand, while SCLC languished, King's national and international reputation grew. *Time* magazine accorded him a laudatory cover story. He was showered with awards, medals, and honorary degrees. President Kwame Nkrumah invited him to Ghana's Independence Day ceremonies. In 1957 he met Vice President Richard M. Nixon and in 1959, President Dwight D. Eisenhower. During his visit to India, Prime Minister Jawaharlal Nehru invited him to dinner—even agreeing to postpone the event when King arrived a day late. In New York, Averell Harriman and Nelson Rockefeller, rivals for the governorship and men of legendary wealth, treated King like a visiting dignitary.

King's appeal to Africans and Indians is obvious enough, but why did conservative white Americans accord him such honor? It is instructive to compare King's soaring prestige in the late 1950s with the fate of two older black leaders, Paul Robeson and W. E. B. Du Bois. Robeson, a great singer and actor, was also a lifelong civil rights activist whose political sympathies lay firmly with the left. As the Cold War hotted up, he made outspoken attacks on American foreign policy, including a speech in Paris in which he stated that in the event of war with the Soviet Union, he would urge blacks not to fight. From that day on Robeson was a marked man. White vigilantes, aided and abetted by the police, broke up one of his open-air concerts. Congressional committees hauled him over the coals. The State Department confiscated his passport. The FBI tailed him. His professional career in the United States was ruined.

Du Bois, the foremost black intellectual of the twentieth century—writer, poet, journalist, sociologist, historian, philosopher, NAACP founder, and uncompromising opponent of racism— went through a similar ordeal. Like Robeson, he suffered for his support of presidential candidate Henry Wallace, who ran against Truman in 1948 on a platform of cooperation with the Soviet Union. In 1951, at the age of 82, Du Bois was indicted as a Communist agent, and was arrested, handcuffed, and fingerprinted; the government withheld his passport. In a symbolic act of defiance, he joined the Communist Party in 1957. Three years later he moved to Ghana. He died in 1963, a virtual exile.

King, by contrast, seemed the perfect black leader for an America still embroiled in the Cold War and traumatized by McCarthyism. Posing as a nonpolitical, nonpartisan advocate of gradual, limited reform, he appealed to the traditional symbols of Americanism: the Bible, the Constitution, the Declaration of Independence, the "American Dream." He defined the racial problem in the narrow terms of "civil rights" or equality under the law, concepts that downplayed the mass poverty afflicting African Americans. His program for social and economic improvement amounted to little more than self-help: "[The African American] must develop habits of thrift and techniques of wise investment; . . . he must act now to lift himself up by his own bootstraps." King's criticisms of capitalism were mild and cerebral; save for vague calls for "nonviolence," he rarely commented on foreign policy. Small wonder he was acclaimed by liberals as well as many conservatives. King was "no radical," *Time* assured its readers— even his taste in suits was "conservative."[8]

It was all a far cry from the class-conscious, socialist-oriented radicalism of the 1930s and 1940s. Battered survivors of the Old Left who still kept the faith found the King phenomenon difficult to comprehend. Some regarded his acceptability to powerful whites as evidence that he functioned, like Booker T. Washington fifty years earlier, as a tool of the white establishment: a safe, flattering, pliable black "leader." It might even be argued, more plausibly, that the more enlightened elements of American capitalism were utilizing King in order to facilitate certain limited but necessary reforms. In the postwar world racism was intellectually discredited and also, in an era of superpower competition and decolonization, politically embarrassing. Economically, the South's rigid caste system was a historical relic, a semifeudal remnant in a society already approaching postindustrialism. Even as it suppressed the Old Left, therefore, the federal government began to withdraw its support from the more blatant forms of racial discrimination, a policy most clearly stated in *Brown* v. *Board of Education.*

Such a crude and schematic analysis, of course, caricatures the historical process. The white elite was itself divided. Many conservatives, like Eisenhower, were extremely skeptical about using federal law to compel white southerners to abandon their traditional "folkways." And big business was generally disinclined to take any initiatives in race relations—to a great extent it had learned to live with, and even profit from, segregation and discrimination. The political system itself, with its checks and balances, separation of powers, and decentralization, has always favored organized minorities, and there was no more determined and politically skilled minority than the white South. The southern oligarchy, its power magnified by black disfranchisement, virtually nullified the *Brown* decision and produced deadlock in Congress. Pressure from African Americans, not elite whites, pushed the civil rights agenda forward.

To depict King as a tool of the ruling elite, moreover, is to overlook the deliberate calculation that determined his political stance. His advisors Rustin and Levison realized that SCLC had to adapt to the political realities of the 1950s: the Old Left had expired; the Democrats had moved rightward; the Cold War was a fact of life. Even self-described liberals gave little thought to the race issue and, when they did, often deplored the "extremism" of the NAACP. In a conservative political climate King had to seek support from across the political spectrum, and this entailed abjuring radicalism and projecting a moderate, nonpartisan image. "The central issue of race relations would become confused and compromised," Levison warned him, "by allowing it to become tied to the many political issues a party deals with simultaneously." King was also advised to shun groups that had been tainted by the McCarthyite witch-hunts. He began to include condemnations of Communism in his speeches.[9]

In negotiating political pitfalls, Levison and Rustin rendered invaluable help. Speaking to Levison after King's death, Rustin recalled that "[i]n the very early days, we by speech writing for Martin created the direction for him." Yet King assessed their advice with a critical mind, accepting or rejecting it as he saw fit. "The man was very independent," remembered Levison. "It was not we directing him so much as we working with him and giving expression to ideals we knew he had or would quickly accept." King and the ministers of SCLC readily understood the tactical advantages of a nonpartisan, "nonpolitical" approach. It was obvious, too, that any hint of radicalism would damage their cause; a strong Christian image, they believed, would make segregationist allegations of Communism less credible.[10]

King, then, would allow himself to be used if he thought it advanced his cause. The events of 1960–62, however, confirmed the danger of mistaking prestige for power, and of confusing symbolism with real leadership. To his discomfiture, King found himself being overtaken by events initiated by others. And to his disgust, he learned that for all the honeyed words of northern politicians his influence over the federal government was nil. In 1963, after a painful reassessment of where he stood, King launched a series of blistering demonstrations in Birmingham, Alabama, which marked a turning point for the civil rights movement.

King's role in the 1960 presidential election underscored the strengths and the limitations of his position. In September 1960 a group of black students in Atlanta laid plans for a sit-in at the restaurant of the Rich's department store. They intended to emulate the tactic pioneered by four students in Greensboro, North Carolina, who, on February 1, 1960, sat down at a "white only" Woolworth's lunch counter and asked for coffee. Though they were denied service, the four remained seated until the store closed; they came back day after day, with more students each time. Their protest inspired black college students all over the South to sit in at lunch counters and restaurants. About seventy thousand people took part in the sit-in movement, and at least four thousand were arrested. Despite being taunted, provoked, and sometimes roughed up, the students exhibited perfect nonviolent discipline.

King applauded the sit-ins but appeared more concerned with lobbying the presidential candidates, Richard M. Nixon and John F. Kennedy, than participating himself. Nevertheless, pressed by the students—"They literally shamed him into getting involved," said one colleague—he reluctantly agreed to join the Atlanta sit-in. On October 19, 1960, he and fifty-one others went to jail.[11]

After the other prisoners were released on bail, however, King was hauled before state judge Oscar Mitchell in DeKalb County, an Atlanta suburb with few blacks and a reputation for being a Klan stronghold. Two months earlier, this same judge had sentenced King to a year in jail for driving in Georgia with Alabama license plates, but the sentence had been suspended. He now meted out four months hard labor, to begin immediately, on the grounds that King had violated his probation.

In the early hours of October 26 the police drove King to Reidsville state prison 230 miles away. Alone, bewildered, and afraid he might not leave prison alive, King wrote a plaintive letter to his wife.

> This is the cross that we must bear for the freedom of our people. So I urge you to be strong in the faith, and this will strengthen me. . . . I have the faith to believe that this excessive suffering that is now coming to our family will in some little way serve to make Atlanta a better city, Georgia a better state, and America a better country. Just how I do not yet know, but I have the faith to believe it will. If I am correct then our suffering is not in vain.

Two days later, however, King was released after Judge Mitchell decided to grant bail after all. It transpired that Robert Kennedy, the younger brother and campaign manager of the Democratic candidate, had made a highly improper but nonetheless persuasive phone call to Judge Mitchell. John Kennedy himself had telephoned Coretta King, then six months pregnant, to express his concern.[12]

The Kennedy campaign team milked this intervention for all it was worth, distributing millions of leaflets in black neighborhoods contrasting Kennedy, "the candidate with a heart," with " 'no-comment' Nixon." The publicity surrounding the incident, and Kennedy's enthusiastic endorsement by Daddy King, contributed to a late shift toward Kennedy among black voters. In an extremely close election, it helped tip the balance toward the Democratic candidate. Thus, King inadvertently became a kingmaker.

If King's prestige helped to decide the election, it did not, however, translate into political influence. In John Kennedy's eyes, his razor-thin majority of 112,000 votes and the loss of Democratic seats in Congress loomed much larger than the black support he had received. While blacks argued that they had supplied the decisive votes, Kennedy attached greater significance to his victory in the southern states, with their overwhelmingly white electorates. Having regained the South after three successive presidential elections in which the Democrats had fared poorly in the region, the retention of southern support became Kennedy's major political priority. Inside Congress, moreover, the influence of the southern Democrats dwarfed that of the half-dozen blacks from the North. The Senate, for example, did not include a single African American, while such southern segregationists as James Eastland of Mississippi and Richard Russell of Georgia chaired key committees. Without the cooperation of these powerful men, Kennedy believed, he had little chance of implementing his policies. Although recognizing the need to consolidate his black support, he had no intention of alienating southern whites and felt no particular debt to King.

Primarily interested in foreign policy, Kennedy displayed little sensitivity to the problem of racism, viewing the civil rights issue as a minor irritant. According to Harris Wofford, his civil rights advisor, Kennedy never took the time "to talk through the issues, or to look ahead and set long-term priorities." His civil rights program could best be described as minimalist. He proposed little in the way of legislation, and that little he did not press hard. Eschewing major reforms, Kennedy proposed to combat discrimination through executive action. So deeply did federal spending and federal regulation penetrate the economy that the President could, in theory, mount a sweeping attack on discrimination using the inherent power of his office. At the same time, the administration planned to expand the black vote in the South by filing suits in federal court, under civil rights legislation passed in 1957 and 1960, against some of the counties with the worst records of disfranchisement.[13]

The executive action strategy enabled the president to bypass Congress, hence its attraction, but it embodied a fatal contradiction. The very existence of the policy testified to the power of the southern Democrats, and whenever vigorous enforcement clashed with white protests, politics ensured that enforcement lost out. The policy itself, moreover, left large areas of discrimination untouched. It did not tackle segregation in public accommodations (restaurants, lunch counters, hotels, and so on). It did nothing to speed up school desegregation, leaving enforcement in the lap of the federal judiciary. It failed to prevent whites from crushing black protests through arbitrary arrests, police brutality, mob violence, and Klan terror. And in the field of voting rights, Robert Kennedy's Justice Department adopted a litigation strategy in spite of the fact that *Brown* had underlined the ineffectiveness of litigation.

The dismal statistics of school desegregation testified to the bankruptcy of relying on the courts to bring about racial change: the stress on voluntary compliance, assumption of white good faith, and acceptance of "tokenism" encouraged white resistance and rendered the process of integration virtually meaningless.

By 1960 only 4,308 black children—0.1 per cent of the black school population—attended formerly all-white schools in the eleven southern states. In the Deep South—South Carolina, Georgia, Alabama, Mississippi, and Louisiana—segregation remained intact. Even apparent victories often turned out to be illusory. The Little Rock crisis of 1957, in which President Eisenhower employed paratroopers to enforce a court order, resulted in the admission of nine black children to one white high school. The following year Governor Orval Faubus closed the city's four high schools, and when they reopened in August 1959 only six blacks were permitted to attend school with whites. In New Orleans the following November, four black girls entered two white elementary schools to the accompaniment of jeering white parents. All the white children withdrew from one of the schools; only a single white child was left in the other. Kennedy's decision to adopt a legal-administrative approach to civil rights, leaving the political power of the South unchallenged, presaged more of the same: reform at a snail's pace.

Federal policy and the emerging civil rights movement were on a collision course. In the student sit-ins of 1960 young African Americans explicitly rejected the legalistic gradualism that had dominated reform during the 1950s. For the first time nonviolent direct action spread throughout the South, and the students used confrontational tactics that entailed deliberate civil disobedience. "This is a new stage in the struggle," Rustin and Levison wrote King. "It begins at the higher point where Montgomery left off." [14]

With the formation of the Student Nonviolent Coordinating Committee (SNCC, pronounced "snick") in 1960, this new stage assumed organizational form. Founded with King's support but prizing its independence, SNCC infused the civil rights movement with a new ethos. Clad in the denim overalls of the rural poor and working round-the-clock for paltry and irregular pay, SNCC's young "field workers" established movement enclaves in the most resistant and dangerous areas of the South, especially Mississippi. Their courage, audacity, and determination soon became legendary. In the face of beatings, shootings, imprisonment, and even death, they refused to give up. And bearing the full brunt of Mississippi's repression, they soon exposed the futility and contradictions of Kennedy's civil rights policy. The federal government urged them to channel their energies into voter registration, yet it disclaimed any power to shield them from violence and arrests. The Department of Justice focused on litigation, but when it attempted to force Walthall County, Mississippi, to register blacks as voters, a Kennedy-appointed judge threw legal obstacles in the government's path. At best, the Kennedy administration was tinkering around the edges of white supremacy; at worst, it was conniving in the very system it purported to oppose. Yet the SNCC workers were in Mississippi to stay: the violence would get worse.

The Freedom Rides of May 1961 brought the Kennedys face-to-face with their first civil rights crisis. Carrying the banner of the Congress of Racial Equality, a group of blacks and whites set out from Washington to ride across the South aboard Greyhound and Trailways buses. They sat as an integrated group and attempted to use all the terminal facilities along the way. Mobs in Alabama beat the riders senseless and burned one of the buses, but students from Nashville, and then from all over the United States, headed south to continue the protest. There were more beatings in Montgomery, and a mass meeting presided over by King found itself trapped inside a church surrounded by a white mob. Kennedy sent U.S. marshals to secure the church, and then federalized the Alabama National Guard to ensure that the Freedom Rides could continue without violence. The riders were arrested in Jackson, Mississippi, for "breach of the peace," and most of them refused bail—a tactic recently devised by the sit-in movement.

The Kennedy administration tried to end the protests. On May 24, as more busloads of Freedom Riders set out for Jackson, Robert Kennedy phoned King to express his disapproval of the "jail-no-bail" tactic. Filling the jails would not have "the slightest effect," he warned, and attempts to embarrass the government would backfire. King pleaded with Kennedy to sympathize with what they were doing:

It's difficult to understand the position of oppressed people. Ours is a way out—creative, moral and nonviolent. It is not tied to black supremacy or to Communism but to the plight of the oppressed. It can save the soul of America. You must understand that we've made no gains without pressure and I hope that pressure will always be moral, legal and peaceful. . . . I'm deeply appreciative of what the administration is doing. I see a ray of hope, but I am different from my father. I feel the need of being free now!

Kennedy was unmoved. "They don't understand the social revolution going on in the world," King told a friend, "and therefore they don't understand what we're doing." [15]

Yet CORE's daring tactics—critics dubbed them "kamikaze" tactics, although nobody died—forced the government's hand. The NAACP had been attempting to desegregate interstate travel through litigation for two decades; despite clear Supreme Court rulings, buses and trains had remained segregated. As a direct result of the Freedom Rides, however, the Interstate Commerce Commission outlawed segregation effective November 1, 1961. The sit-ins and the Freedom Rides provided King with powerful examples of nonviolent direct action. They challenged his imagination and posed a test of his leadership. Unless he responded to this new level of militancy, his symbolism would soon wear thin. At the end of 1961, King became embroiled in his first campaign of civil disobedience.

5

Confrontation: Albany and Birmingham

On December 14, 1961, King received a telegram from Dr. William G. Anderson, a black osteopath, urging him to "come and join the Albany Movement." King arrived in the southwest Georgia town having promised to make a speech. But he stayed to lead a march, was arrested and jailed, and found himself embroiled in a remarkable protest movement.

The Albany Movement owed its existence to Cordell Reagon and Charles Sherrod, two young SNCC workers who hoped to instigate the kind of audacious tactics pioneered by the sit-ins and the Freedom Rides. At first, only students and young people took them seriously, but their flamboyant behavior soon made older blacks sit up and take notice. The pair engineered a series of dramatic incidents at the bus and train stations to show that the city was still enforcing segregation, despite the new federal edict on interstate travel. The ensuing arrests angered the black community, and hundreds protested by marching to city hall under the banner of the Albany Movement, a coalition of black organizations that Dr. Anderson had agreed to head. The city council was determined, however, to maintain segregation. The police arrested nearly five hundred marchers and insisted on a cash bond of $100 from each person—money that many could not pay. Black leaders felt they were in over their heads, and some were losing their nerve. They hoped that King would be able to retrieve the situation.

Looking around the crowded pews of Shiloh Baptist Church on December 15, King could see an impressive cross section of Albany's black community: old men in creased blue overalls, professionals in white shirts and ties, maids and housewives, students and schoolchildren. He could sense the "movement spirit," that magic ingredient that inspired ordinary people to do extraordinary things. It was almost palpable in the emotional atmosphere of the packed church and, above all, in the extemporized verses and simple, powerful melodies of the "freedom songs," which had titles like "Ain't Gonna Let Nobody Turn Me 'Round" and "I Woke Up This Morning with My Mind Set on Freedom." King also heard a stirring rendition of "We Shall Overcome." SNCC workers had learned this union song, which had started life as a hymn, in 1960. Sung slowly with improvised counterpoints and swelling harmonies, it soon became the anthem of the civil rights movement. The Albany Movement reminded King of the inspiring early days of the Montgomery bus boycott: here was a ready-made movement—enthusiastic, apparently united, and eager to bestow its leadership on him.

King seized the moment. "Don't stop now," he urged his audience at the end of a riveting speech. "Keep moving. Walk together children, don't you get weary. There's a great camp meeting in the sky." The following day, accompanied by Dr. Anderson and Ralph Abernathy, his friend and colleague from SCLC, King headed a slow, quiet procession toward city hall. All 257 marchers were arrested for "parading without a permit." King vowed to spend Christmas in jail, and the staff of SCLC embarked on a frantic campaign to drum up national support and publicity.

To King's dismay, however, the campaign of direct action rapidly fell apart, and all his subsequent attempts to achieve a clear-cut victory proved unavailing. In August 1962, after two more spells in jail, he left Albany as segregated as he had found it. Whites had failed to yield any ground whatever. What went wrong? Among the many factors that conspired to frustrate the Albany Movement, two stand out: disunity, and the guile of chief of police Laurie G. Pritchett.

The emotional response that greeted King's arrival disguised a welter of factionalism among the blacks who composed the leadership of the movement. The lines of division and suspicion ran this way and that, strangling the prospects for unity. Part of the problem lay in organizational rivalry. When it learned of SNCC's presence in Albany, the NAACP instructed its local officials to cold-shoulder SNCC's efforts to form a united front. This narrow sectarianism typified the NAACP's attitude to other civil rights groups. But SNCC's dealings with King betrayed similar pettiness. Struggling to establish its own identity, SNCC acquiesced in Dr. Anderson's invitation to King but resisted the notion of surrendering the leadership to him. Some of the locals who headed the Albany Movement also developed misgivings about King's role; they especially resented the assertive manner of Wyatt T. Walker, whom King had recruited as SCLC's executive director. Oblivious to these tensions, King had to deal with the fact that Dr. Anderson, in jail with him, showed signs of succumbing to mental stress.

The upshot was a debacle that verged on farce. Egged on by Ella Baker, who had left SCLC in 1960 belittling King as a "prophetic leader who turns out to have heavy feet of clay," the SNCC workers prevailed upon Marion Page, Anderson's deputy, to show King the door. On December 17 Page told reporters that the Albany Movement needed no "outside help"; the next day he agreed to call off the demonstrations in return for the release of the imprisoned marchers. King emerged from jail, alongside Anderson, to find that Page had settled for the flimsiest of concessions. Local whites gloated as he left Albany; newspaper reports of his departure read like obituaries.

Characteristically, King swallowed his humiliation and refused to engage in recriminations. Returning for his trial on July 10, 1962, he reentered the campaign, determined to salvage something from the fiasco of December. For the next month his presence invigorated the protests: blacks marched in the streets, prayed on the steps of city hall, boycotted the downtown stores, and conducted sit-ins at white-only restaurants. And when SNCC workers mocked him as "De Lawd," berated him for his caution, and chastised him for being "bourgeois," King reciprocated with endless patience. He and the others in SCLC were older men, he explained; they had families and mortgages and were bound to be more conservative. "We would like to think that you are the creative antagonists who make this sort of situation, and that we . . . come in and help you work in them." SNCC tolerated King's intervention because local blacks adored him, and his presence secured much-needed publicity. As one SNCC worker conceded, King could "cause more hell to be raised by being in jail one night than anyone else could if they bombed city hall."[1]

At every point, however, King's tactics backfired, and the enthusiasm of the black population began to flag. When King chose to spend forty-five days in jail rather than pay a $178 fine, the mayor of Albany surreptitiously paid the money, forcing the astonished prisoner to walk away free. Inevitably, some blacks muttered about King turning "chicken." As he struggled to regain the initiative, the campaign stalled once again when the city authorities obtained an injunction against further marches from federal judge Robert Elliott. Over the strenuous objections of SNCC, King insisted on obeying the court order. The chief judge of the federal appeals court, Elbert Tuttle, soon voided Elliott's injunction, but an outbreak of rock- and bottle-throwing by some blacks persuaded King to further delay the resumption of demonstrations. The protests finally got underway again, and King spent two weeks in jail after another arrest. But the campaign's momentum had been irretrievably lost. When he left jail after receiving a suspended sentence, he also left Albany.

Whites could thank Laurie G. Pritchett, chief of police, for King's discomfiture. The fat, drawling Pritchett looked like the archetypal southern cop, but his calm, canny handling of the demonstrations defied the stereotype. As an efficient police chief who discouraged brutality, Pritchett understood the political dimensions of the challenge posed by black protests. The danger to segregation, he realized, lay not so much in the pressure of demonstrations but rather in the possibility of direct federal intervention in southern affairs. And he perceived—more keenly than King at this stage—that nothing would encourage federal intervention more surely than a violent response to nonviolent protest. Pritchett's strategic approach was to read King's account of the Montgomery bus boycott, *Stride Toward Freedom,* which gave him valuable insight into the thinking of his adversary, and to consult other police chiefs who had succeeded in containing black protests. The plan was clear: a policy of arresting demonstrators, applied firmly but without violence, would obviate federal intervention and suffocate nonviolent protests. During the first half of 1962, anticipating King's return, Pritchett drilled his men: "At each roll call they were lectured and shown films on how to conduct themselves."[2]

As King and SCLC licked their wounds, they pondered the lessons of the campaign. On the one hand, the movement in Albany represented a significant escalation of the civil rights struggle. For the first time, an entire black community had been mobilized for a broad attack on segregation, and large numbers of ordinary people—not only students—had gone to jail. On the other hand, Albany painfully illustrated the limitations of nonviolent direct action. In India the British had been a tiny minority. In every southern state, blacks were clearly outnumbered; in Albany they constituted only a third of the population. Moreover, because most blacks depended upon white employers, relatively few, five percent at most, were prepared to risk jail. Talk of a "nonviolent army" that would "fill up the jails" had been exposed as wishful thinking. King's army had been pitifully small, and Pritchett ensured a plenitude of jail space. By countering civil rights demonstrations with the repressive machinery of the law, the white authorities turned the contest into a war of attrition that blacks could not win.

In such an unequal contest, only strong intervention by the federal government could tip the scales in favor of the weaker protagonist. In May 1962 King called upon President Kennedy to issue a "Second Emancipation Proclamation," urging him to throw the full weight of his office behind the struggle for black civil rights. Kennedy did not seriously entertain the idea, and he avoided entanglement in the Albany situation. Instead, Robert Kennedy, as Attorney General, sought to dissuade King from pressing the demonstrations; while critical of the city's refusal to negotiate, Kennedy tacitly endorsed its restrained, low-key handling of the protests. The administration's "neutrality" infuriated the normally equable King. Arguing with Kennedy over the phone, he complained that the government had no comprehension of what blacks in Albany were up against. "This can't go on," he insisted. "I'm tired. We're sick of it."[3]

Reflecting upon the government's inaction, King arrived at an uncomfortable conclusion: shallow political considerations, not reason or morality, guided the administration's actions. If a crisis threatened political embarrassment, if violence and disorder got out of hand, then the government would indeed intervene. If, however, southern racists quietly stifled black protests, then it acquiesced in the status quo. This seemed to be the lesson of the Freedom Rides. In Alabama, where the white authorities had summoned up the Klan to brutally assault the protesters, Kennedy acted in a most forceful manner, but when the Mississippi authorities simply jailed the Freedom Riders, ensuring that no mobs gathered, the government did nothing. Evidently, the absence of overt violence in Albany made it a minor local difficulty that could safely be ignored. The crisis at "Ole Miss" in October 1962 underscored the point. When the entry of James Meredith, an African American, into the University of Mississippi prompted rioting by white segregationists—violence that left two people dead—Kennedy sent in troops.

Hardened by defeat, King decided to explode the political equivalent of a bomb under the federal government. He would launch demonstrations in Birmingham, Alabama.

The sheer audacity of King's decision was astonishing. Birmingham now prides itself as a model of racial harmony; it even boasts a museum that honors the civil rights movement. In 1963, however, Birmingham exemplified all that was extreme, vicious, and violent in southern racism. Founded by aggressive capitalists after the Civil War, Birmingham was a coal and steel center that possessed none of the genteel ways and paternalistic traditions of older cities like New Orleans or even Montgomery. In the 1930s Birmingham experienced bitter industrial conflict and saw the emergence of a militant labor movement. But the city disproved the notion that racism and capitalism were antithetical: rigid segregation characterized industry as well as public life, and the white union branches provided a steady stream of recruits for the Ku Klux Klan. Indeed, Birmingham boasted some of the most dangerous Klan groups in the South.

Above all, Birmingham meant Theophilus G. "Bull" Connor, who bore the ironic title Commissioner of Public Safety, a post that included supervision of the police and fire departments. First elected in 1937, Connor became friendly with the city's industrialists but also retained his popularity with white workers. Connor was a fervent racist and his publicity-conscious and high-handed actions to defend segregation outraged northern liberals but delighted Birmingham's white voters. In 1938 he insulted First Lady Eleanor Roosevelt. Ten years later he arrested a U.S. senator. By the late 1950s he had become a law unto himself, and his methods had become increasingly thuggish. He used his control of the police force to tap telephones, spy on meetings, and frame opponents. With the protection and cooperation of the police, the Klan bombed black churches, brutally assaulted the Freedom Riders, and castrated a black man for the sheer hell of it. Birmingham became so notorious for racial violence that a group of whites framed a new city charter that abolished Connor's job of public safety commissioner. When voters approved the change, Connor decided to run for mayor.[4]

The Reverend Fred L. Shuttlesworth emerged as Connor's most forceful and determined black opponent. Impulsive, excitable, and egocentric, Shuttlesworth almost single-handedly kept black protest alive in Birmingham after the suppression of the NAACP in 1956. Intent on integrating the most segregated city in the South, he was blasted out of bed by dynamite, beaten up by white mobs, and repeatedly arrested by Connor's police. The diminutive clergyman displayed a bravado that amused blacks and caused them to shake their heads in admiration and amazement. The organization he built up over the years, the Alabama Christian Movement for Human Rights, was the strongest of the local groups that made up SCLC. With several hundred devoted followers and a handful of ministers he could count on, Shuttlesworth provided SCLC with a solid base upon which to build its campaign.

King started with several advantages. In Albany he had stumbled into a protest not of his making and not under his control; the white authorities had been able to keep him off-balance. In Birmingham he would not be plagued by divided and confused authority, and he would begin with the element of surprise. Whereas in Albany the whites had put up a solid front of resistance, in Birmingham they were split between the hardliners, who backed Connor for mayor, and the moderates, who preferred the more conciliatory Albert Boutwell. King also had a team behind him. Wyatt Walker, the clergyman hired in 1960 to breathe life into SCLC, provided the drive, discipline, and administrative talent that the more easygoing and reflective King sometimes lacked. With Shuttlesworth's advice, Walker drafted a detailed campaign plan that identified targets, specified tactics, and dealt with the minutiae of recruiting demonstrators.

A small group of organizers assisted Walker. Andrew Young, thirty-one years old, came from New Orleans; his ordination in the mainly white Congregational church made him something of a rarity among black ministers, but it gave SCLC important contacts with the white clergy. Young had the organizational know-how to function as Walker's number two, and he also possessed the social and diplomatic skills to negotiate with southern whites. James Bevel, who was in his early twenties, had none of Young's social polish but possessed far more experience at the grass roots of the civil rights movement; as a veteran of the sit-ins and the Freedom Rides, he had spent two years in Mississippi. Although he was a rabble-rousing orator, Bevel regarded himself as an expert on Gandhian tactics. He had picked up many of his ideas from James Lawson, a Methodist minister and articulate intellectual who had been expelled from Vanderbilt University for his role in the Nashville sit-in movement. In Birmingham Lawson developed a program for training demonstrators in nonviolence. Dorothy Cotton, who normally worked in SCLC's citizenship education program, worked alongside Lawson and also performed more general duties. Two other staff members answered directly to King. Ralph D. Abernathy, King's best friend, served him as companion and troubleshooter. Bernard Lee, a young man, acted as King's secretary, bodyguard, and general factotum. No rigid lines separated these roles. SCLC had no armchair generals or deskbound bureaucrats: everyone pitched in.

King had two broad objectives in Birmingham. The first was to force white leaders to begin the process of desegregation. He regarded the precise scope of any agreement as unimportant; any concessions, however small, would constitute a victory. In order to achieve a victory, therefore, King focused on the desegregation of Birmingham's downtown department stores, a relatively narrow goal. Fred Shuttlesworth was unhappy with such a limited objective, but King did not want to risk the failure of an overambitious assault against segregation across the board. As Walker recalled, "We knew that as Birmingham went, so went the South. And we felt that if we could crack that city, then we could crack any city." Learning from Albany, however, King realized that it would be useless to demand concessions from the city government, which could not afford to lose face in the eyes of the largely white electorate. SCLC therefore ensured that its primary demand, the desegregation of department store eating facilities, could be satisfied with or without the agreement of white politicians. The pressure of demonstrations, underpinned by a black boycott of the city's downtown shopping district, would force the city's businessmen to the negotiating table.[5]

A negotiated settlement, however, also depended on SCLC's second goal, federal intervention. In order to bring about federal action King had to tread a very fine line. Without the restraining influence of national publicity, which carried the possibility of federal interference, the white authorities would feel free to suppress the demonstrations with whatever force they deemed necessary. King was counting on the news media to inhibit Bull Connor from employing his customary brutality. But King also had to discredit Connor in the eyes of the nation, thus embarrassing the government into assuming responsibility for ending the crisis. He had to make Connor show his true colors, but without provoking bloodshed.

The resolution of this paradox lay in King's use of symbolism. Although he sought a confrontation between demonstrators and police, he envisaged a tightly controlled one that strove for dramatic effect rather than physical conflict. One journalist likened the campaign to a carefully staged morality play, and this was precisely the effect King intended. The campaign had to maintain a sense of momentum and drama: the demonstrations needed to build up to a powerful climax. Walker tried to anticipate every contingency so that SCLC could retain the initiative.

But everything about the Birmingham project was risky. King would be charged with extreme provocation, especially as white moderates were attempting to drive Connor from office. Nor could King count on black unity. Many middle-class blacks were appalled by the prospect of King, an outsider, mounting demonstrations with Shuttlesworth, whom they considered an irresponsible firebrand, at the very time that Connor was becoming discredited and the political situation balanced on a knife-edge. Lest they tip the balance to Connor in the imminent mayoral election, SCLC prepared for the campaign in secret, which severely limited the opportunity to mobilize black support in advance. Blacks in this tough steeltown, moreover, would look upon nonviolence with puzzlement and cynicism; many possessed guns and routinely carried knives. The possibility of a bloodbath, which would discredit not only Connor but King as well, could not be discounted. As he faced the supreme challenge of his career, King somberly warned his colleagues that some of them might not leave Birmingham alive.

At first little went according to plan. Although Boutwell won more votes than Connor in the mayoral election, King had to further delay the campaign because a runoff was necessary for Boutwell to achieve the required overall majority. When the protests finally began on April 3, 1963, few people volunteered for jail, and many blacks, including leading ministers and businessmen, openly criticized the campaign. King had anticipated black opposition, but its depth took him by surprise. Many resented having been kept in the dark and felt that King should allow Boutwell a honeymoon period. King had to spend a week rallying black support—although he was careful not to admit that SCLC's refusal to permit another delay stemmed from its eagerness to confront Connor, who through legal strategems was clinging to his post as Commissioner of Public Safety.

Connor declined to play the role that SCLC's script assigned him, however. The Birmingham police exhibited uncharacteristic restraint and were content simply to arrest all demonstrators for "parading without a permit." Even so, and despite King's exhortations, few people joined the marches. The mass meetings were enthusiastic enough, but fear of arrest and loss of employment deterred most blacks from walking down the aisle to the front of the church when King's aides appealed for volunteers. With the campaign apparently coming undone, the prospect of either negotiations or federal intervention seemed remote.

The campaign soon reached a crisis point: King needed to lead a march and go to jail in order to revive media interest and stimulate black support. There were also reasons, though, why King should stay out of jail. The city authorities had obtained a blanket injunction against the demonstrations, and King had never hitherto disobeyed a court order. Moreover, SCLC had exhausted its bail fund, and at a tense strategy meeting many argued that only King could raise enough money to get the incarcerated demonstrators released. Ralph Abernathy lamely argued that he could not accompany King to jail because he had to preach the Easter Sunday service at his Atlanta church. Daddy King implored his son not to march. King withdrew to a side room in order to pray. When he rejoined the anxious group, he was wearing denim jeans and a rough work shirt—his prison clothes. Colleagues later cited the decision as evidence of the religious inspiration that guided King; the day of his arrest, Good Friday, invested it with additional symbolism. Yet King's "faith act" was never really in doubt. He had long ago resolved to break any injunction issued by the Alabama courts, knowing that an appeal to the federal courts would entail years of litigation.

King dreaded solitary confinement. Separated from Abernathy after his arrest on April 12, "those were the longest, most frustrating and bewildering hours I have lived," he remembered. "You will never know the meaning of utter darkness until you have lain in such a dungeon, knowing that sunlight is streaming overhead and still seeing only darkness below." A gregarious man, he hated being alone. He ached to see his new daughter, born a few days earlier. He worried about the bail money. And he experienced straightforward fear. In New York Stanley Levison speculated that Connor was trying to "break" King. Walker, too, feared for his safety and advised an anxious Mrs. King to make direct contact with the president. Coretta King's messages eventually reached Robert Kennedy, who returned her calls. Connor was "very difficult to deal with," the attorney general explained. Nevertheless, he assured her of the administration's concern. The following day, President Kennedy added his own reassurances. "We sent the FBI into Birmingham last night," he divulged. "We've checked on your husband, and he's all right."[6]

A few minutes later, King's jailers allowed him to take a telephone call from Coretta. The news of Kennedy's conversation with his wife surprised and pleased him. It gave the campaign a "new dimension," he believed. Guessing correctly that Connor had the line tapped, he told Coretta to immediately inform "the Reverend" (Wyatt Walker) of Kennedy's intercession. The administration's concern for King's safety did not imply active intervention. Well aware that King was trying to force his hand, Kennedy had no intention of being drawn in against his will; indeed, he disclaimed any legal authority for involvement. Nevertheless, the government found the situation in Birmingham disturbing. "The Negro population has no confidence at all in the local police," one official advised Robert Kennedy. "And there is no doubt but that a good number of Negroes carry weapons."[7]

King also received the welcome news that singer Harry Belafonte, a staunch supporter, had managed to raise $50,000 in bail money. But an additional worry now nagged at King. White moderates, whose support he desperately wanted, were displaying little sympathy for the protests. They criticized the timing and the tactics of the campaign, and some questioned King's motives. Over the years King had become hardened to criticism, but attacks from southern churchmen saddened, irritated, and finally angered him. Reading the local newspaper in his cell, he came across an open letter signed by eight of Alabama's most respected white clergymen. Denouncing the demonstrations for inciting hatred and violence, their statement praised the conduct of the police, called for negotiations between "local leaders," and urged blacks to shun King's campaign.

Depressed, and then furious, King penned a rebuttal, filling up the margins of the newspaper with his spiky handwriting. In what amounted to twenty impassioned pages he castigated the eight clergymen for their superficial analysis, rebuked self-styled white moderates for their "shallow understanding," and charged the white church with hypocrisy and lack of moral commitment.

At the core of "Letter from Birmingham City Jail" was the most systematic exegesis of civil disobedience that King ever gave. He called upon such diverse authorities as Socrates, the Old Testament prophets, Thomas Aquinas, and Martin Buber to testify in his defense. He likened himself to Saint Paul, another "outsider," and Jesus, another "extremist." He frankly avowed that his demonstrations sought to create "tension" and "crisis," but insisted, with a bow to Niebuhr, that only pressure could induce privileged groups to act justly. Besides, he pointed out, "We merely bring to the surface the tension that is already alive." He denied the charge of provocation, arguing that blacks were not to be blamed if whites responded to their peaceful protests with violence. And he bluntly warned of a "frightening racial nightmare" if blacks surrendered to bitterness and hatred because whites refused to negotiate with responsible leaders like himself.

King also employed pathos, describing the pain he felt seeing the impact of discrimination upon his own children.

> You suddenly find your tongue twisted and your speech stammering as you seek to explain to your six-year-old daughter why she can't go to the public amusement park that has just been advertised on television, and see the tears welling up in her eyes when she is told that Funtown is closed to colored children, and see ominous clouds of inferiority beginning to form in her little mental sky, and see her beginning to distort her personality by developing an unconscious bitterness toward white people. . . . [Y]ou have to concoct an answer to a five-year-old son who is asking: "Daddy, why do white people treat colored people so mean?"

King's polemic had no influence on the campaign. But when "Letter from Birmingham City Jail" was published it soon became the most widely-read, widely-reprinted and oft-quoted document of the civil rights movement. It was the most powerful and influential piece of writing that King ever produced.[8]

When King left jail after nine days, he stood trial for violating the state court injunction. Judge William Jenkins recognized that

King behind bars was an embarrassment to the city: instead of jailing him for civil contempt until he apologized to the court, he found him guilty of criminal contempt only. The latter carried but a short sentence, and King would remain free during the lengthy appeals process. This moral victory, however, did not help King. The white authorities were still handling the demonstrations gingerly. Although the old city government was exploiting legal technicalities to cling to power, the courts would soon confirm Boutwell's election and Connor would be out of office. Without Connor, the chances of engineering a dramatic confrontation with the police would fade. The press were already losing interest in the demonstrations, whose ranks were dwindling. Walker began delaying the start of the daily marches so that large crowds of black bystanders gathered: their presence conveyed an illusion of mass support. But the illusion would soon wear thin unless SCLC recruited more demonstrators.

James Bevel suggested a way of doing just that. He proposed going into the city's black schools to enlist children in their thousands. The magnitude of such a step worried King: at what age should SCLC permit children to join the demonstrations, and should they allow children to take part if the parents objected? By the end of April children as young as nine were going to jail, but only with their parents' permission. Recruiting them en masse was a different proposition. It would not only incur the opposition of many parents but also in all likelihood be perceived by the outside world as cowardly manipulation. Nevertheless, King tacitly encouraged Bevel to organize a mammoth demonstration composed of schoolchildren. On May 2, which Bevel dubbed "D-Day," thousands of black children deserted their classrooms and converged on the Sixteenth Street Baptist Church, the gathering point for demonstrators. Leaving the church in groups of fifty, they walked into the arms of waiting policemen to be hauled away in paddy wagons. About six hundred went to jail that day, and by May 7 well over two thousand were in custody.

The "children's crusade" finally made Connor snap. Angered by the crowds of black spectators that were becoming bigger and bolder each day, he told the police to utilize German shepherds to keep them in check. He then ordered the fire department to disperse the throngs with their high-pressure hoses. The press had a field day; the scenes were broadcast across America and around the world. Overnight, the black community united behind the protests: so many people came to the mass meetings that it took four churches to accommodate them all. King could hardly contain his joy. "This is the most inspiring movement that has ever taken place in the United States of America," he told a packed church on May 5. "There are those who write history, there are those who make history, there are those who experience history. . . . You are certainly making history and you are experiencing history. And you will make it possible for the historians of the future to write a marvellous chapter. Never in the history of this nation have so many people been arrested for the cause of freedom and human dignity."[9]

Sickened and embarrassed by the spectacle and fearful of a racial explosion, President Kennedy asked his brother to bring the two sides together. On May 3 Robert Kennedy's most talented mediator, Burke Marshall, arrived in Birmingham with instructions to halt the descent into chaos. A week later, after tense and exhausting negotiations, and the application of direct pressure by the president and attorney general, a committee of white businessmen accepted some of the movement's demands. The principal concession appeared slight: department stores agreed to desegregate their eating facilities and hire black sales assistants. But King had achieved his goal and also played his last card. Untrained in nonviolence, the black crowds were becoming unruly, and he could not contain the violent elements much longer. Claiming victory, he ended the demonstrations. But as the protests stopped in Birmingham, African Americans poured into the streets all over the South. King had unleashed the biggest wave of black militancy since Reconstruction.

6

March on Washington
to Selma

In an age when rifles, tear gas, and riot shields are standard police gear, it is difficult to recapture the horror with which Americans viewed the actions of Bull Connor in the early days of May 1963. Americans of all persuasions, from President Kennedy down, deplored Connor's tactics. Almost overnight, white segregationists found themselves on the defensive. In vain did southern congressmen argue that dogs and firehoses constituted normal crowd-control techniques: northerners likened the Birmingham police to Nazi storm troopers and Soviet border guards.

It was indicative of the comparative domestic tranquility of the late 1950s and early 1960s that the scenes in Birmingham evoked such an outcry; after all, no demonstrators died and few sustained serious injuries. The condemnations also testified to the dramatic quality of the confrontation between police and demonstrators. Photographs of blacks parrying snarling German shepherds and being hurled against walls by stinging jets of water adorned the front pages of newspapers around the globe. Television images had even greater impact. Virtually every contemporary commentator stressed the extraordinary power of the newsreels. As Kennedy himself noted, the "shameful scenes" in Birmingham were "so much more eloquently reported by the news cameras than by any number of explanatory words." The fact that television news was still in its infancy made the images from Birmingham all the more vivid and influential. (Ironically, King himself seems to have underestimated this new medium—perhaps because he had so little time to watch television—being more concerned with the newspaper reports.)

The effect of the Birmingham incident on African Americans was electrifying. The sight of young black children coolly defying Connor's police amazed and inspired them; the mass arrests and use of dogs and firehoses infuriated them. This volatile mixture of anger and inspiration exploded in a wave of protest, as reservoirs of fear suddenly drained away. No longer were protests confined to college students, isolated communities, or small groups of dedicated activists. Throughout the South, blacks marched through the streets in acts of calculated defiance; people of all ages and occupations joined in the protests as the emotion of the hour submerged old divisions and momentarily banished doubts about King's tactics. The fervor for direct action also gripped the NAACP, prompting Roy Wilkins to join a picket line in Jackson, Mississippi, whence he was carted off to jail. "We've finally baptised brother Wilkins," King joked. Each day saw fresh demonstrations and confrontations. By the end of the summer of 1963, blacks had marched by the hundreds of thousands. About twenty thousand people were arrested.[1]

King sensed a historic breakthrough. Never before had he seen such unity and militancy among southern blacks: nonviolent direct action had come of age, with blacks organizing spontaneously across the South. Birmingham had transformed the political climate, raising the issue of civil rights to a prominence it had never before commanded. It was vital, King thought, to step up the pressure on the federal government, not only by demonstrating in the South but also by raising the protest to a national level. According to conventional political wisdom, strong civil rights legislation would never get through Congress. King believed that it could, however, if the administration made a strong enough commitment: "We need the President to do crusading work for us." At the urging of younger staff members such as James Bevel, he proposed a massive demonstration in Washington, a "march on Washington" of perhaps a quarter of a million people, a powerful, visible expression of black militancy in the heart of the nation's capital.

King's plan appalled the Kennedy administration. White shame over Birmingham soon turned into apprehension as black protests escalated during the summer. In such an explosive situation, when the South teetered on the brink of anarchy and violence, it seemed the height of folly to assemble hundreds of thousands of African Americans in Washington and then harangue them with angry speeches. President Kennedy implored King to abandon the idea, warning that if pushed too far, demonstrations might lead to bloodshed and damage the blacks' cause. Kennedy was also alarmed by the radicalization of black opinion, as well as embarrassed by the damage to America's international reputation. Previously opposed to strong legislation, he now viewed it as essential in order to head off black extremism and to end street protests.

On June 11, in a televised speech to the nation, President Kennedy finally made the commitment that King had so long urged upon him. Deploring the fact that racial discrimination still perverted the ideal of equality under the law, the President proposed new legislation to tackle the "moral crisis" confronting America. The Civil Rights Bill he sent to Congress on June 19 was sweeping. He sought more power for the federal government to desegregate southern schools, combat discrimination in employment, and end black disfranchisement. Above all, he wanted a blanket ban on segregation in public accommodations, including hotels, restaurants, theaters, and shops. Would it not be sensible now, Kennedy asked King, to desist from demonstrations until Congress had passed this Bill?

King's interest, however, lay in prolonging the crisis. Convinced that only the pressure of direct action had induced the administration to act, he unashamedly exploited the government's alarm. His message became harsher; warnings of violence and extremism became more explicit. In "Letter from Birmingham City Jail," he had warned that black nationalist groups were "springing up across the nation," and that their rise, unless checked, would cause the streets of the South to be "flowing with blood." As Congress debated the Civil Rights Bill, he repeatedly invoked the specter of black nationalism, with its connotations of antiwhite violence, in urging whites to support the bill. He now posed nonviolence as an *alternative* to violence.

To conservatives, such warnings were demagogic threats of the most irresponsible kind. King's nonviolence, they argued, carried the implicit threat of violence and amounted to a despicable form of political blackmail. King rejected such accusations, and felt acutely uncomfortable forecasting violence. Nevertheless, he appreciated that his growing influence among whites stemmed, at least in part, from their growing fear of black extremism and their perception that by supporting King they might contain black anger within manageable bounds. King subtly exploited white anxieties, particularly current concerns about the Nation of Islam, whose members were popularly known as "Black Muslims," a group that shunned whites and wanted nothing to do with King's doctrine of nonviolence. Growing racial tension made whites increasingly sensitive to the "reverse racism" of black fringe groups, and the Muslims had an able propagandist in Malcolm X, eloquent and charismatic lieutenant of Elijah Muhammed, the sect's reclusive founder. White liberals were fascinated and appalled by Malcolm's quick wit and chilling characterization of whites as "snakes" and "devils." By escalating direct action, King would compel northern whites to support his own Christian, nonviolent, integrationist reformism out of sheer fear of the alternative.

It was a dangerous strategy. Most demonstrations were calm and dignified, but sometimes discipline broke down under police provocation. How long could black leaders keep up the protests while maintaining nonviolent order? For King, however, the opportunities far outweighed the dangers. By resorting to direct action blacks in the South had regained the initiative and broken the political deadlock that had paralyzed the federal government. Moreover, King had become so identified with direct action that his reputation stood or fell by its success. Above all, he realized that the geometric growth of black militancy was a phenomenon of such elemental force as to defy the control of any individual leader or group of leaders. It was "like an ocean tide," recalled Andrew Young. "You might direct it constructively. . . . But for us to stand in the way and say 'stop this'—we would have been swept away." [2]

King gambled on his ability to stimulate direct action while keeping black protests within the bounds of nonviolence. In urging blacks to boycott and demonstrate, he not only stressed the futility of violence but also ceaselessly expounded on the virtues of love—not "emotional bosh," he explained, not "affectionate love or friendship," but the kind of unselfish love defined by the Greek word *agape.*

Agape is understanding, creative, redemptive goodwill for all men, it is the love of God operating in the human heart. It is an overflowing love which seeks nothing in return. . . . Love is a willingness to go the second mile in order to restore the broken community. Yes, love is even a willingness to die on a cross in order that others may live.[3]

On a more practical level, King recognized the necessity for caution and compromise. He discouraged provocative tactics. He cut short protests that threatened to degenerate into disorder. He tried to avoid demoralizing, embittering defeats, even if it meant accepting face-saving truces. He was also sensitive to the need for political tact. In 1964, for example, he agreed to a moratorium on demonstrations during the presidential election campaign.

This painstaking effort to combine militancy and moderation was not merely sound strategy: King had a profound ethical commitment to seeking a responsible "middle way" between unacceptable extremes. But it involved continual compromises that exposed him to incessant criticism. The younger activists of SNCC and CORE complained that King encouraged blacks to take action but then either failed to follow through on promises of help or settled for meaningless paper victories. They considered King's belief in white good faith naïvely misplaced and complained that deliberately or unwittingly, he allowed himself to be used by the federal government as a restraint on black protest. Many regarded King's injunction to love the white oppressors demeaning; black psychologist Kenneth B. Clark even termed it "pathological." Conservatives in the NAACP believed that King's publicity-seeking demonstrations hampered the more important tasks of litigating through the courts and lobbying Congress.

Between 1963 and 1965, however, King's dogged pursuit of moderate militancy earned him a key position in the loose, broad coalition that assembled around the goal of racial equality. He not only provided black Americans with their most effective collective voice but also expressed the ideals of racial equality better than any other person. Idolized by blacks as the embodiment of courageous protest and admired by white liberals as the symbol of racial reconciliation, King managed to position himself in what a contemporary observer termed the "vital center" of the civil rights movement. Balancing right and left, black and white, old and young, he provided these disparate elements with a focus for unity, a fulcrum that gave them maximum political leverage.[4]

The March on Washington exemplified King's ability to unify and project the civil rights movement. Originally conceived by A. Philip Randolph as a two-day protest to dramatize unemployment among blacks, King picked up the idea amid radical talk of bringing the capital to a standstill. The march that actually took place, however, on August 28, 1963 entailed neither direct action nor marching. Instead, it was a day-long rally of about 200,000 people, including a large number of whites, in support of the Civil Rights Bill. SNCC disparaged the absence of direct action and the emphasis on interracialism and political moderation. And it was bitter that some of the white speakers had pressured John Lewis, SNCC's chairman, to tone down his criticism of the Kennedy administration. Without King's commitment to legal protest and legislative reform, however, the NAACP would have boycotted the event, white religious leaders would not have participated, and the massive turnout could not have been achieved.

The Lincoln Memorial, the march's backdrop, held a special significance for African Americans. When it was dedicated in 1922 whites viewed it as a symbol of national unity rather than a celebration of Lincoln the Great Emancipator. Over the following decades, however, blacks used the Lincoln Memorial as a powerful symbol of freedom, linking their struggle against discrimination with a great work of monumental architecture in the nation's capital. In 1939 the black opera singer Marian Anderson had performed on the steps of the memorial when the Daughters of the American Revolution denied her the use of Constitution Hall. In 1957 King spoke at the monument at a "Prayer Pilgrimage" organized by SCLC and the NAACP, making an eloquent plea that southern blacks be allowed to vote. Now, six years later, on the centenary of Emancipation, King echoed the words that were engraved on the base of Lincoln's statue in a speech that became as famous as—if not more than—the Gettysburg Address. "Five score years ago," he began, "a great American, in whose symbolic shadow we stand today, signed the Emancipation Proclamation. . . . But one hundred years later, the Negro still is not free."

The speech he delivered at the March on Washington was in some ways untypical: it conveyed little of the sheer force of King's oratory in the more intimate settings of church services and mass meetings. Even so, it is fitting that it remains his most celebrated public statement. "I Have a Dream" encapsulated King's message and appeal. On the one hand, he lauded the "marvellous new militancy that has engulfed the Negro community," warning that the "whirlwinds of revolt" would "continue to shake the foundations of our nation." On the other hand, King described his dream of reconciliation and racial harmony:

I have a dream that one day this nation will rise up and live out the true meaning of its creed, "We hold these truths to be self-evident, that all men are created equal." I have a dream that one day on the red hills of Georgia, sons of former slaves and sons of former slaveholders will be able to sit down together at the table of brotherhood. I have a dream that one day even the state of Mississippi, a state sweltering with the heat of injustice, sweltering with the heat of oppression, will be transformed into an oasis of freedom and justice. I have a dream that my four little children will one day live in a nation where they will not be judged by the color of their skin, but by the content of their character. I have a dream today! I have a dream that one day down in Alabama . . . little black boys and black girls will be able to join hands with little white boys and white girls as sisters and brothers. I have a dream today!

King framed this vision entirely within hallowed symbols of Americanism: the Bible, the Declaration of Independence, the Constitution, the Emancipation Proclamation, and the "American Dream". The refrain of the patriotic song "My Country 'Tis of Thee" led to his peroration:

> "From every mountainside, let freedom ring." And when this
> happens, and when we allow freedom to ring, when we let
> it ring from every village and every hamlet, from every state
> and every city, we will be able to speed up that day when all
> God's children, black men and white men, Jews and gentiles,
> Protestants and Catholics, will be able to join hands and sing
> in the words of the old Negro spiritual: "Free at last. Free at
> last. Thank God almighty, we are free at last."

King's performance enraptured the vast assemblage. Even southern whites, who could view the proceedings on television, grudgingly praised the dignity of the occasion.[5]

King's schedule became more hectic than ever as he wrestled with the demands of writing, fund-raising, speechmaking, lobbying, pastoring, administering, planning, and campaigning. According to one estimate, he delivered 350 speeches during 1963, travelled 275,000 miles and spent nine days in ten away from home.

The six weeks between May 26 and July 2, 1964, illustrated the breakneck pace of King's life. After two days in St. Augustine, Florida, a picturesque tourist town where Ku Klux Klan pressure had prevented any integration, he flew to New York to address the NAACP Legal Defense Fund. He then embarked upon a western fund-raising trip that included five stops in California and Arizona. In Los Angeles, learning that marchers in St. Augustine had been attacked by a white mob, he telegraphed President Johnson to request federal intervention. Speaking by phone to federal officials, he pointed out that the strength of the Klan, plus the delinquency of the local police, made further violence inevitable. He also reported numerous threats against his life—adding that this was nothing unusual and that he was not seeking special protection. On June 4 he returned to St. Augustine but departed the following day for New York. There he spoke at two universities, appeared on a television program, had a private meeting with Republican Senator Jacob Javits, and consulted Bayard Rustin, Clarence Jones, Harry Wachtel, and the other advisors who composed his research committee.

Arriving back in St. Augustine on June 10, he was arrested the following day at a white-only motel, summoned to testify for three hours before a local grand jury, and then driven to a jail in Jacksonville, Florida, where he spent the night in solitary confinement. Bailed out on June 13, he flew north to deliver a college commencement address, collect an honorary degree from Yale University, and attend a meeting to discuss the forthcoming Democratic National Convention, when blacks from Mississippi, under the banner of a SNCC-sponsored Freedom Democratic Party, planned to challenge the legality of the official "lily-white" delegation. Back in St. Augustine on June 16, King rejected calls for a thirty-day "cooling-off" period, insisting that whites appoint a biracial committee before demonstrations ceased. After two days of meetings and speeches in Chicago, and a session with the research committee in New York, King flew back to St. Augustine, spent a weekend in Atlanta, and then returned once again to Florida in an effort to find a way out of the stalemate.

It is no small wonder that King felt overwhelmed by problems; he confessed that "sometimes the pressures get so great that you are forced to do things you don't believe you should do with hindsight." The St. Augustine protests ended inconclusively, but King was philosophical, reasoning that "some communities, like this one, have to bear the cross."[6]

When President Johnson signed the Civil Rights Act on July 2, 1964, the civil rights movement could celebrate a major victory. Segregation in public facilities (parks, libraries, hospitals) and public accommodations (stores, restaurants, motels) became illegal. Employers could no longer lawfully discriminate on the grounds of race, color, sex, or ethnic origin. The government could initiate suits to desegregate southern school districts, as well as cut off federal funds to districts that proved recalcitrant.

But black gains stirred powerful white hatreds and resentments. The civil rights movement hardly had time to consolidate its advance before confronting a racist counterattack. This onslaught had diverse elements and took three broad forms: a political challenge to the leadership of the Democratic and Republican parties; a campaign of terror against the civil rights movement in the South; and an effort to discredit King personally.

Black leaders expected die-hard opposition from southern whites. Opposition from northern whites, to whom they looked for political support, was a different matter. When evidence appeared of a "white backlash" in the North they became seriously concerned, and when the racist governor of Alabama, George C. Wallace, took his campaign for the Democratic presidential nomination to Indiana and Wisconsin, attracting a third of the vote, their concern turned into alarm. King considered Wallace "perhaps the most dangerous racist in America today."

The nomination of Senator Barry Goldwater as the Republican candidate in the 1964 presidential election posed an even greater threat. The choice of Goldwater was a repudiation of the moderate Republicanism espoused by Eisenhower in the 1950s. The defeated contender, Nelson Rockefeller of New York, headed the party's liberal Eastern wing; he warmly supported the civil rights movement. Goldwater, the political darling of doctrinaire conservatives, whose strength lay in the South and West, condemned the Civil Rights Bill as socialistic—he was one of only six Republicans to oppose the bill when it finally passed the Senate on June 19, 1964. King warned that a Goldwater victory would spark "violence and riots . . . on a scale we have never seen before."

Although this twin threat from the right gave black leaders the jitters, the center managed to hold. After the shock of President Kennedy's assassination on November 22, 1963, a desire for reconciliation dominated the national mood. Lyndon B. Johnson, Kennedy's successor, skillfully exploited this yearning for consensus, using his southern origins and vast congressional experience to pilot the Civil Rights Bill through Congress with wide bipartisan support. Moreover, the Right suffered from disunity. Unless it could rally around a credible candidate, it would be doomed to minority status. Both Wallace and Goldwater repelled moderate conservatives, and Goldwater waged a campaign of such ineptitude that he split his own party, guaranteeing a Democratic victory. Ostensibly nonpartisan, King campaigned for Johnson. "We were just scared to death of Goldwater," Andrew Young recalled.

The spread of black protests, the passage of the Civil Rights Bill, and Johnson's election added up to a major defeat for the South's political leaders, who by and large had pursued a policy of peaceful resistance. Opposition to integration had been spearheaded by local "Citizens Councils," comprising the white elite, and had employed litigation, economic coercion, and political pressure. As the Citizens Councils declined, however, more violent elements came to the fore, and between 1963 and 1965 the Ku Klux Klan experienced a major revival. On September 15, 1963, Klansmen planted a bomb at the Sixteenth Street Baptist Church in Birmingham; the explosion killed four young girls. In 1964, as SNCC prepared to send a thousand volunteers, mostly northern white students, to Mississippi, white racists organized the White Knights of the Ku Klux Klan. On June 21 they murdered three civil rights workers, two of them whites. On July 11 Klansmen in Georgia killed a black school administrator. In 1965 the Klan carried out murders in Alabama, Mississippi, and Louisiana. Whenever the accused killers stood trial, white juries acquitted them.

The Department of Justice claimed it was powerless to act. If local juries failed to convict defendants accused of murder, a state rather than a federal crime, there was nothing it could do. And if local officials failed to stop racist violence the same argument applied. Law enforcement was a local responsibility: the federal government had no police force and could not possibly use troops to occupy the South.

The civil rights movement rejected these arguments as sophistries and denounced the government for tolerating a reign of terror. How could blacks depend on the state authorities to curb violence when the local police included members of the Klan and governors like George Wallace cultivated Klan support? Black leaders argued that the federal government possessed both the means and authority to act but lacked the political will. They were especially incensed by the role of the Federal Bureau of Investigation, whose agents merely stood by taking notes while blacks and civil rights workers were beaten and arrested. King shared this anger and frustration. He repeatedly criticized Kennedy and Johnson for refusing to intervene in racial trouble spots. And he attacked the FBI for sympathizing with the southern segregationists, fraternizing with the local police, and failing to apprehend Klan bombers and murderers.

King's criticisms incensed the FBI's director, J. Edgar Hoover, who initiated a vicious campaign to discredit King. His motive for attacking King, however, went far beyond a desire to protect the bureau's public image. The aging director, head of the FBI since 1924, was identified in the public mind as the nemesis of gangsters and desperadoes, but his primary concern lay in combatting left-wing radicalism. The Cold War boosted his authority over "internal security," and by the 1950s he had turned the FBI into a political police force that used surveillance, phonetapping, informants, forgery, breaking and entering, and other "dirty tricks" to destroy left-wing organizations. Basking in his reputation as an authority on subversion and scourge of Communists, Hoover consistently magnified the influence of the moribund Communist Party. His definition of a Communist, moreover, was infinitely elastic, and he stretched it to include virtually anyone to the left of his own reactionary views. When it came to race, he instinctively sympathized with the white South and fought stubbornly to keep the FBI out of civil rights cases. He insisted that under no circumstances would the bureau protect civil rights workers.

Appalled by the rise of the civil rights movement, Hoover singled out King, its primary symbol, as the man to stop. Pressed by their boss to link King with Communism, Hoover's underlings swallowed their doubts and echoed the expected line. "We are in complete agreement with the Director that communist influence is being exerted on Martin Luther King," reported a senior official on September 25, 1963, adding that his "powerful, demagogic speech" at the March on Washington revealed King to be "the most dangerous and effective Negro leader in the country." Three months later, the FBI devised plans "aimed at neutralizing King as an effective Negro leader." At the appropriate time, it intended to "expose King as an immoral opportunist who is . . . exploiting the racial situation for personal gain."[7]

Stanley Levison unwittingly paved the way for this covert campaign of denigration, disruption, and blackmail. Learning that Levison had become one of King's advisors, Hoover warned Robert Kennedy that a top Communist was a member of King's intimate circle. Without questioning Hoover's characterization of Levison, the attorney general authorized an FBI wiretap on his telephone. The tap provided a plethora of information about Levison's role as fund-raiser, speechwriter, and confidante, enabling Hoover to bombard Kennedy with reports about his sinister "influence" over King. Taking Hoover's allegations at face value, Robert Kennedy urged King to repudiate Levison, and on June 22, 1963, the president himself took King aside in the White House Rose Garden to reinforce this advice. Very reluctantly, King agreed to sever his relationship with Levison. When the wiretap revealed, however, that the break was not complete, Hoover requested and received permission to tap King's own telephones, as well as those of two other advisors, Bayard Rustin and Clarence Jones.

Was Levison a Communist? The most knowledgeable authority, David J. Garrow, claims that he had been closely involved in the Communist Party's financial affairs in the early 1950s. Although the FBI never furnished credible evidence to this effect, Garrow believes that the bureau's reticence stemmed from its concern to protect the identities of two highly-placed informants. It has been suggested that Levison himself might have been an FBI plant, but the transcripts of his wiretapped telephone conversations, released in 1983 under the Freedom of Information Act, make this theory highly implausible. Perhaps Levison *was* a secret Communist who laundered Moscow's gold. Or perhaps he was merely a freelance radical who mixed with Communists during the 1930s and 1940s and then defended them during the McCarthyite witch-hunts. The FBI could easily clear up the mystery, but it still declines to do so. In the absence of a smoking gun, therefore, a firm conclusion about Levison's alleged Communist affiliations is impossible.[8]

Whatever the answer, two points are clear. First, if Levison had ever been in the Communist Party, by the time he became an advisor to King he had broken with it. Second, the notion of a wily Levison manipulating a naïve King is nonsense—the FBI could only create such a fantasy by doctoring the evidence of its own wiretaps, which graphically illustrated King's sturdy independence. For the FBI, Levison was merely a convenient weapon with which to attack King.

By the end of 1963 King was caught in an intricate surveillance web. In addition to wiretaps, the FBI planted numerous illegal hidden microphones in King's hotel rooms. This eavesdropping not only yielded a flow of political intelligence that the FBI used to impede King's activities but also threw a light on the private man that convinced Hoover that he could "destroy the burrhead."

The precise nature of the FBI's notorious King tapes remains obscure. The conversations recorded from King's own telephones are sealed under federal court order until 2027, and the whereabouts of the illicit recordings are unknown—doubtless they have long since been destroyed. Not surprisingly, the FBI learned that away from the public spotlight, unwinding with a few close colleagues, King sometimes became inebriated and enjoyed bawdy jokes. What else it learned is a matter of speculation. Allegations about King's sexual promiscuity are still confined to the realm of innuendo and must be treated with caution. Although Hoover described King as "a 'tom cat' with degenerate sexual urges," one must remember that the FBI director was a lifelong bachelor, widely rumored to be homosexual, who harbored a prurient interest in other people's sex lives.

In the cultural context of his time, King's far-from-spotless private life was not particularly unusual. The unofficial mores of the era sanctioned male adultery, especially by the powerful and famous, in a way that they no longer do. The liaisons of Presidents Roosevelt and Eisenhower and the inveterate womanizing of President Kennedy never became public knowledge during their lifetimes. Newspaper editors had a gentlemen's agreement to suppress such information—no one would touch the FBI's King material. In addition, black ministers engaged in their own conspiracy of silence. To many of the women who made up the bulk of his flock, the black preacher exerted a strong sexual attraction. Illicit relationships were commonplace; preachers treated them as subjects of amusement rather than reproach. Given this tolerant sexual climate and his extended absences from home, King's infidelity becomes explicable. There also seems to have been something, however, in King's psychological makeup that made him see attractive women as potential conquests. King seemed incapable of being monogamous. But in the absence of personal letters, frank reminiscences, or "kiss-and-tell" biographies, it is difficult to assess the significance these extramarital affairs held for him.

Throughout 1964 the FBI sought to discredit King. Hoover's agents briefed journalists, churchmen, politicians, and top government officials (including President Johnson) about King's "immorality" and supposed Communist sympathies. They tried to undermine his public appearances, hamper his fund-raising, and block his awards and honorary degrees. The FBI even attempted to dissuade foreign leaders, including Pope Paul, from receiving him. King's prestige merely increased, however. In January *Time* named King its "Man of the Year"; in October he won the Nobel Peace Prize, the youngest person ever to receive that honor. Hoover was appalled, commenting that "top alley cat" would be a more appropriate prize. On November 18, 1964, frustrated by his failure to dent King's public image, Hoover publicly attacked him as "the most notorious liar in America," adding off the record that he associated with Communists and was "one of the lowest characters in America." Three days later, the FBI mailed King a tape recording with an accompanying note that virtually invited him to commit suicide. "There is but one way out for you," the note concluded. "You better take it before your filthy, abnormal fraudulent self is bared to the nation."[9]

King felt astonished, angry, and frightened. Curbing his initial inclination to blast Hoover as a senile incompetent, he decided to appease his tormentor. A meeting with the director on December 1 passed with excruciating politeness but entirely avoided the matter of Hoover's blatant campaign of character assassination. When King received the tape recording in early January, Andrew Young and Ralph Abernathy raised the matter with a Hoover assistant only to elicit a barefaced denial. King felt helpless. "We couldn't possibly take on the FBI with its 6,000 agents and millions of dollars," Young recalled. President Johnson, moreover, obviously knew about Hoover's attacks but did nothing to stop them.[10]

Yet King weathered the storm. Hoover no longer commanded the adulation he had enjoyed during the heyday of McCarthyism. Civil rights leaders rallied to King's defense, attacking the FBI's record in the South and deploring Hoover's comments; they even visited the White House to protest to Johnson. The President's own silence over the affair did not necessarily indicate support for the FBI director, despite the fact that he had just reappointed him. It was common knowledge that even presidents felt intimidated by Hoover's voluminous files. As Johnson once commented, it was better to have him "inside the tent pissing out than outside the tent pissing in." By continuing to grant King personal access, however, Johnson signalled that he had not been influenced by Hoover's antics. The very nature of the FBI's salacious "evidence," moreover, posed a problem for Hoover. How could he publicize such material without incriminating himself? And how could skeptical journalists be convinced of the authenticity of muffled noises on dubious tapes? Coretta King's loyalty also helped save King: a separation or divorce would have inflicted untold damage on his reputation. In today's moral climate, when the private lives of politicians and public figures are considered fair game, King might not have survived.

The FBI persevered in its efforts to besmirch King's reputation and undermine his plans. They undoubtedly exacted an emotional and psychological toll. "They are out to get me, harass me, break my spirit," he complained. He could never be sure, moreover, about the scope and effect of FBI disruption. Dissension might be the result of agents provocateurs. Mishaps might have been caused by FBI dirty tricks. Declining income might stem from FBI efforts to hamper SCLC's fund-raising. Negotiations might fail because the other side was privy to King's strategy. Critical news stories might have originated with the FBI's Crime Records Division. False rumors might have been planted by the bureau's Counterintelligence Program.[11]

King and SCLC learned to live with FBI harassment and even to joke about it. A poor telephone connection elicited complaints that the FBI man was causing interference and could he please get off the line. From time to time, King would sneak up on FBI agents, introduce himself, and thank them for their "protection." If a colleague made a crude remark, King joked that he had just earned himself membership in Hoover's "Golden Record Club." Whenever Ralph Abernathy found a microphone hidden under a pulpit, he pretended that Hoover was listening at the other end. "It got to be a crowd-pleasing routine," said Andrew Young. "He'd pick it up . . . and he'd preach to it." King and his colleagues reasoned that their movement was an open one; it had nothing to hide. Attempting to evade FBI surveillance would not only be futile, it would also lead to paranoia and paralysis.[12]

Refusing to be cowed, King travelled to Selma, Alabama, at the beginning of 1965 to launch a new campaign of nonviolent direct action. Despite the fact that most southern blacks were still denied the vote—one of the crucial flaws in the 1964 Civil Rights Act—President Johnson told him that it would be unrealistic to expect further legislation so soon. King disagreed: "We will seek to arouse the federal government by marching by the thousands. . . . We must be willing to go to jail by the thousands. We are not asking, we are demanding the ballot." [13]

King had selected his target with care. In Selma whites made up ninety-nine percent of the voters but less than half the population. In some nearby counties not a single black person voted although blacks heavily outnumbered whites. King had also picked suitable adversaries. Sheriff Jim Clark was an unvarnished racist who, with his roughneck posse, delighted in terrorizing "uppity niggers." Behind Clark loomed Governor George Wallace, uncompromising opponent of the civil rights movement and sworn political enemy of President Johnson.

In a series of notes he wrote to Andrew Young from a Selma jail cell, King encapsulated his tactical mastery of nonviolent direct action. "Please don't be too soft," King told Young on February 4, 1965. "We have the offensive. It was a mistake not to march today. In a crisis we must have a sense of drama." [14]

At each stage of the Selma campaign King upped the ante, escalating the protests in scope and daring. He began by lining up prospective voters outside Selma's courthouse, then instigated "illegal" marches, resulting in mass arrests. After leaving jail he organized simultaneous demonstrations in surrounding counties; then night marches; and then, after state troopers shot and killed a black man as they violently dispersed a demonstration, he endorsed the idea of a fifty-mile march from Selma to Montgomery.

On Sunday, March 7, six hundred demonstrators left Selma heading toward the state capitol in Montgomery. On the outskirts of the town, state troopers and mounted sheriff's deputies drove them back using clubs, whips, tear gas, and brute muscle. Although King did not participate in the march—and was widely criticized for his absence—news cameras captured the entire incident. Americans across the nation, witnessing the scene on television, were outraged. President Johnson was already considering voting rights legislation, but the reaction to Selma's "Bloody Sunday" made up his mind. SCLC had dramatized the unfairness of black disfranchisement to such effect that Johnson went before Congress to ask for a voting rights bill, vowing that "this time, on this issue, there must be no delay, no hesitation, no compromise." Praising the courage of the demonstrators, Johnson astonished his audience and moved King to tears by invoking, with deliberate emphasis, the anthem of the civil rights movement: *"And we shall overcome."* Passed in August 1965, the Voting Rights Act swept away all the discriminatory tests and ruses that whites had employed to stop blacks from voting. It paved the way for the emergence of a truly democratic South, one in which blacks could vote without let or hindrance; one in which blacks could hold political office and exercise power alongside whites. It was the crowning achievement of the civil rights movement.[15]

For ten years King had inspired black southerners with hope. As they marched and protested in the face of overwhelming odds, he constantly assured them that God, history, and America were on their side. Despite setbacks like Albany, King translated this fusion of religious faith and democratic idealism into a powerful sense of self-confidence and historical momentum. By 1965 it seemed that the civil rights movement had finally evoked a solid national consensus in favor of racial equality. President Johnson's deployment of federal troops to protect the march from Selma to Montgomery symbolized this commitment: never before had the national government identified itself so completely with both the goals and methods of the civil rights movement. As he addressed twenty-five thousand people before the steps of Alabama's statehouse, King felt great joy and optimism. "We are on the move now," he told them, "and no wave of racism can stop us." [16]

Less than a year after the passage of the Voting Rights Act, however, this mood of hope had vanished. By 1966 the ghettos of the North trembled with anger; civil rights workers renounced non-violence and chanted "Black Power"; whites in the North began openly to express their racial bigotry; America was at war in Vietnam. Buffeted by political and ideological storms, the civil rights movement disintegrated, and King found himself confused, depressed, and isolated.

7

Descent into Chaos

THE CIVIL RIGHTS MOVEMENT had paid little attention to the North, now home to half of the total African-American population. Blacks had migrated to the cities of the North in order to escape the South's grinding poverty and oppressive racism. In the North, according to the law, blacks enjoyed the same rights and opportunities as whites: they could vote, have free access to public accommodations, and attend schools that were theoretically integrated. But in the North, too, pervasive discrimination, sometimes subtle and sometimes blatant, hampered their daily lives. Blacks lived in segregated areas—many of them slums—and usually attended all-black schools. Their communities were ravaged by crime, drugs, and unemployment. "Urban renewal," moreover, was destroying many of the older, more stable black neighborhoods—blacks were being uprooted and funneled into ugly public housing projects to make way for civic centers and expressways. Everywhere, blacks felt the sting of insensitive and often brutal white policing.

Despite numerous state laws requiring fair employment practices, racial discrimination was especially rife in the job market, relegating most blacks to the bottom rungs of the economic ladder. In the construction industry it was virtually impossible for blacks to obtain a union card. Police and fire departments were practically all-white. Factory jobs, which had lured blacks North in the first place, were increasingly scarce. Although the North boasted a sizeable black middle class—mainly teachers and federal employees—most blacks worked in the lowest-paid and least secure sectors of the economy. Black unemployment was permanently high, at least double the white unemployment level. Whites virtually monopolized white-collar jobs: there were very few black managers, lawyers, journalists, or university professors.

Although blacks could vote, they were underrepresented; the few black politicians, moreover, proved incapable of articulating their grievances with the necessary urgency and passion. The fiery rhetoric of Malcolm X, however, had resonated throughout black neighborhoods; African Americans applauded the way Malcolm extolled pride in blackness, castigated whites, and denounced nonviolence. In fact, during the last year of his life, after he broke away from Elijah Muhammed's Nation of Islam, Malcolm had renounced his earlier blanket condemnation of white people and tried to find common ground with the civil rights movement. By the time of his murder in 1965 Malcolm had yet to devise a realistic program or strategy for black advancement; it was the earlier, angrier Malcolm who would be remembered and revered. The dramatic successes of the civil rights movement in the South had made northern blacks all the more aware of their poverty, their pariah status, and their inability to break out of the suffocating ghettos, but they had no constructive outlet for their anger and frustration.

The riot in Watts, Los Angeles, in August 1965 underscored the gravity of the situation. There had been riots in New York, Rochester, and Philadelphia the previous year, but Watts dwarfed these outbreaks. The worst urban violence since 1943, the Watts riot lasted six days, ravaged forty-five square miles, led to four thousand arrests, and left thirty-four people dead. It was not only the scale of the violence that staggered America but also its occurrence in leafy and spacious Los Angeles, where such an incident was least expected.

Watts dismayed King. The civil rights movement had been concerned with disfranchisement and segregation in the South; it had never devised a strategy for attacking poverty and had neglected the problems of African Americans in the North. King now had to remedy that enormous omission. He decided to take SCLC to Chicago, in order to demonstrate that the tactics that had worked in the South could be successfully applied in the North. He believed that nonviolent direct action would give blacks both a vent for their anger and an effective means of collective action. It would thus discourage further rioting and bring about tangible improvements in urban conditions.

When King went to Chicago at the start of 1966 to launch the Campaign to End Slums, he felt confident of success. He anticipated the support of Chicago's white liberals, who had enthusiastically backed the southern civil rights movement, and he believed that President Johnson would be sympathetic, for King's plans seemed consonant with the aims of Johnson's recently proclaimed War on Poverty. He did not expect Mayor Richard J. Daley, Chicago's powerful "Boss," to welcome him with open arms but believed nevertheless that Daley would offer concessions once he felt the pressure of a mass movement. King was relying on James Bevel to build a "massive disciplined organization" that would unite black slum dwellers in a grassroots movement. With 100,000 demonstrators at its command, SCLC would be in a powerful bargaining position. "We are going to create a new city," Bevel predicted. "Nobody will stop us." [1]

The following nine months crushed King's optimism, however. In the South he had motivated blacks to take extraordinary risks by equating freedom with the simple right to vote.

In Chicago, where the taste of such "freedom" had long since turned sour, his idealistic rhetoric failed to evoke the same fervent response. King could always attract an enthusiastic audience, but the urban masses observed his efforts with detached cynicism. Bevel's "nonviolent army" failed to materialize; the ranks of King's marches were woefully thin. King even failed to prevent rioting: in July, just as the movement girded itself for demonstrations, a riot erupted in the West Side ghetto, and King proved powerless to stop it.

In the South King had relied upon the crass brutality of his opponents to arouse and unite blacks. He knew that he would be unable to count on such brutality in Chicago. "There will be fewer overt acts to aid us here," he predicted; "naive targets such as the Jim Clarks and George Wallaces will be harder to find and use as symbols." Even so, Daley's slipperiness continually kept him off balance. Welcoming King to Chicago, the Mayor exuded sweet reason and kept his police force under tight control. King struggled to create a sense of momentum and drama, but he found it difficult to gain the initiative. Daley played tricks with him, he complained, agreeing with his goals but doing nothing to further them.

When he finally discovered an effective tactic, it hurt King as much as it hurt Daley. In late July blacks marched into Chicago's white neighborhoods to protest against the racist attitudes and practices that confined blacks to segregated ghettos. The demonstrations certainly dramatized the problem: white residents pelted the marchers with rocks, bottles, and fireworks. Obliged to give the marchers police protection, Daley incurred the ire of his white constituents, who wanted the black intruders stopped. Every time they marched, bragged Bevel, Daley lost a thousand white votes. Each demonstration also weakened King's own white support, however, and as the confrontation neared a climax with a threatened march into Cicero—a literally all-white suburb notorious for its racism—key allies lost their nerve. Catholic primate John P. Cody asked King to halt the protests. Others denounced King's tactics as provocative and self-defeating. They intensified the white backlash, one civic leader complained, and "set back peaceful integration in these neighborhoods many years."[2]

Increasingly isolated, King negotiated the Summit Agreement, which pledged the city and the real estate industry to end housing discrimination. Although King called off the marches, the white signatories failed to follow through on their promises. With the agreement gathering dust, King mounted a voter registration campaign in an effort to shake Daley's grip on the black vote. It was a total failure. In April 1967 Daley easily won a fourth term of office, and blacks voted for him four-to-one. King left Chicago empty-handed.

The Chicago debacle forced King to reassess his basic assumptions about American society. He had always taken it for granted that the South was the bastion of racism; racial discrimination persisted in the North, to be sure, but he had viewed it as a secondary, residual phenomenon. When he led a demonstration through Chicago's Gage Park, however, the howling white mobs shocked and frightened him; he had "never seen anything so hostile and hateful," even in the South. As he told Daley over the conference table, "Our humble marches have revealed a cancer."[3] His discovery of that cancer dented King's faith in American democracy. For ten years he had confronted white Americans with the disparity between their democratic ideals and their undemocratic practices, confident that he could arouse the conscience of "the great decent majority." In Chicago he learned that racism assumed a different form in the North but was no less virulent. Despite the progress of the previous decade, he told his staff, the civil rights movement "did not defeat the monster of racism. We have got to see that racism is still alive in our country. And we have got to see that the roots of racism are very deep."

King also altered his views about racism itself. Blacks were not simply confronting irrational prejudice on the part of individuals but also systematic economic exploitation by the majority. He likened the ghettos to internal colonies: whites controlled and perpetuated them because they profited from them. The movement's demand to end slums, he now realized, had challenged powerful economic interests. "You can't talk about ending slums," he warned his staff, "without first seeing that profit must be taken out of slums. You're really . . . getting on dangerous ground because you are messing with folk then. You are messing with Wall Street. You are messing with the captains of industry." The white backlash, he contended, had only a superficial connection with the spread of black rioting: white racism was coming out into the open because whites saw their privileges being threatened. The backlash was "a reaction to questions being raised by the civil rights movement which demand a restructuring of the architecture of American society."

King confessed that victories like the Civil Rights Act and the Voting Rights Act had misled him. Whites acquiesced in these laws because the blatant violence of the South's caste system offended their sense of fair play, but also because the reforms left existing economic relationships essentially intact. "We must admit it," he told his staff, "the changes that came about during this period were at best surface changes." They did little or nothing for the "millions of Negroes in the teeming ghettos of the North."

King realized that demands for economic equality went well beyond the traditional agenda of American liberalism, but only collectivist solutions, he believed, could eliminate the enormous economic disparity between black and white Americans: "Something is seriously wrong with capitalism." Lecturing to his staff, he cited Sweden as an example of democratic socialism that the United States would do well to emulate: a society without slums, poverty, or unemployment, a society with free health care for all, a society dedicated to peace.

Advisors cautioned him to tread warily. Whites were not ready for "deep radical change," Stanley Levison warned. There might well be scope for improvement within the existing economic system, and it was certainly "poor tactics" to claim that black equality could *only* be achieved "with the revolutionary alteration of our society." Faced with that demand, whites would opt for the status quo even if it perpetuated discrimination. Bayard Rustin agreed with King on the need for radical change but proposed conventional, even conservative, means to that end. Blacks had to move "from protest to politics," working within the Democratic party to strengthen its progressive orientation. King had to be careful, moreover, not to threaten the party's national leadership, particularly Daley and Johnson.[4]

Such arguments no longer convinced King. If the Chicago protests exposed the racism of the big-city machines that dominated the Democratic party, America's growing involvement in Vietnam illustrated the bankruptcy of President Johnson's reformism. By the end of 1966 Johnson had sent four hundred thousand troops to South Vietnam, and American planes were bombing North Vietnam. His pursuit of the war had become an obsession, and his program of domestic reform, the Great Society, ran out of steam. Aware that the white backlash was hurting the Democratic party in the North, Johnson let the 1966 Civil Rights Bill, which proposed a partial ban on housing discrimination, die in the Senate. Johnson, in fact, felt increasingly exasperated by black demands and began avoiding even loyal black supporters. "In the last few weeks," a member of his staff complained in August 1966, "he has not talked to any Negroes at all."[5]

In August 1965 King had made a personal appeal for negotiations to end the war. Deluged by ridicule and criticism, he made a pragmatic decision to drop the proposal, reasoning that he could not press the issue without alienating President Johnson and damaging the civil rights movement. If he continued to involve himself in foreign policy, Rustin warned, critics would come down on him "like a house on fire."

By the end of 1966 King deeply regretted this climb-down. It had neither helped the civil rights movement nor enhanced his influence with Johnson. Throughout 1966, in fact, the president had treated King with studied indifference—when the attorney general argued that a telegram from King merited a personal reply on the grounds that "King is useful to us," Johnson chose to snub him instead. Above all, with Congress hacking away at the War on Poverty, the notion of "guns and butter" had been exposed as a fiction. "The bombs in Vietnam explode at home," King told a Senate committee. "They destroy the hopes and possibilities for a decent America."

Vietnam had also shattered the anti-Communist consensus and King, like many others, now questioned the very basis of America's foreign policy. This war was no aberration, he argued: from its earliest involvement in Indochina the United States had opposed the forces of Vietnamese nationalism, first supporting French colonialism, then sponsoring a puppet regime in the South. When the peasants revolted against this oppression, America sent massive armies to prop up governments that were "corrupt, inept, and without popular support." It was as if, he told his staff, "the French and the British had come here during the Civil War to fight with the Confederacy." The war typified the logic of America's obsession with containing Communism. "The shirtless and barefoot people of the land are rising up as never before," King marvelled. But instead of supporting this revolutionary nationalism, which sought "new systems of justice and equality," America allied itself with corrupt generals, grasping landlords, and rapacious corporations. Communism was an indictment of capitalism's failure. But in Vietnam, throughout Latin America, and wherever its influence extended in the Third World, America defended capitalism by perpetuating neocolonialism. It had become the archreactionary power of the late twentieth century.

Above all, the war revolted King. America, he complained, had become "the greatest purveyor of violence in the world." As if the sheer scale of the violence were not bad enough, America's methods of prosecuting the war were singularly barbaric: massive bombing, "disgusting napalm," the destruction of forests, crops, and villages. American firepower had killed a million civilians, he claimed, "mostly children."

King took nonviolence very seriously. He regarded his Nobel Peace Prize not merely as recognition of his civil rights leadership but also as confirmation that he had a role to play on the world stage. He deeply resented the patronizing way the administration had belittled his 1965 peace initiative, implying that blacks were incapable of discussing complex matters of state. The notion that foreign policy should be left to "experts" struck him as a pernicious, undemocratic doctrine that had contributed to the Vietnam disaster by stifling criticism and dissent. In practice, he well knew, successive administrations had no objection to black leaders speaking out on foreign policy as long as they supported the anti-Communist line.

Throughout 1966 King felt ashamed of his mealymouthed statements on the war, reproaching himself for moral cowardice. He also felt hypocritical preaching nonviolence to blacks in America when he failed to oppose the war in Vietnam—a war in which blacks were fighting and dying "in extraordinarily high proportions." At the beginning of 1967, unable to bear "the betrayal of my own silences," King denounced the war in a series of angry, passionate speeches, and on April 15 he addressed a demonstration outside the United Nations building in New York organized by James Bevel, the first Spring Mobilization Against the War. He even considered running for president as a peace candidate.[6]

King's stock with the government, already low, reached rock bottom. Johnson "flushed with anger," wrote one insider, when he read a summary of "Beyond Vietnam," King's definitive attack on the war. The White House staff hastened to reassure Johnson that most blacks supported the war and that King's influence was fast fading. "He will become the folk hero of the alienated whites," wrote John P. Roche, "but lose his support . . . among the great bulk of the Negro community." King was "inordinately ambitious," Roche added, "and quite stupid." Another assistant revealed that only about a quarter of the blacks questioned in an opinion poll agreed with King's position. In the press the organs that had built King up now turned against him. *Life* described "Beyond Vietnam" as a demagogic slander that sounded like a script for Radio Hanoi." The *Washington Post* dismissed the speech as "sheer inventions of unsupported fantasy," adding that people who had respected King in the past would "never again accord him the same confidence." [7]

In 1967 King felt increasingly pessimistic. The peace movement seemed ineffectual as the war ground on; for the second successive year, Congress rejected a civil rights bill and cut the War on Poverty, and the "long, hot summer" witnessed the worst outbreak of ghetto violence thus far—dozens of riots that left eighty-three people, nearly all of them blacks, dead. In Detroit alone forty-three people were killed, fifteen hundred injured, and five thousand arrested. The riots undermined King's influence with both whites and blacks: with whites, because he had failed to avert violence and may even have encouraged it with his cavalier attitude to the law; with blacks, because violence seemed a more dramatic and satisfying expression of protest and self-assertion.

King viewed the riots as nihilistic, self-defeating outbursts of rage—a disaster for African Americans. They destroyed black neighborhoods and left black people dead; they angered and frightened whites, provoking harsh, repressive countermeasures. But in arguing against violence, King found himself continually on the defensive, for the concept of Black Power lent a romantic aura to the riots and gave a spurious legitimacy to all manner of black extremists.

Black Power began life as a slogan, chanted defiantly by SNCC workers against King's wishes on a march through Mississippi in June 1966. It signaled a repudiation of King's leadership—the rejection of integration as an end and nonviolence as a means to that end. Above all, it marked the end of the idealistic belief that the civil rights movement could depend upon whites to further its cause.

SNCC's disillusionment with whites grew out of its experiences in Mississippi. There, SNCC workers had seen and experienced the most brutal forms of white oppression only to have white liberals—who liked to describe themselves as the "best friends of the Negro cause"—continually criticize them for being too militant, too radical, too unreasonable, too irresponsible. And the Democratic party, which assiduously sought black votes, had betrayed the cause of racial equality at the 1964 Democratic National Convention in Atlantic City. During the Freedom Summer of 1964, SNCC had organized the Mississippi Freedom Democratic Party (MFDP), which represented the state's disfranchised black population but was open to all, regardless of race. The MFDP sent an integrated delegation to Atlantic City, challenging the right of the all-white "official" delegation to represent Mississippi at the Democratic National Convention. At President Johnson's insistence, however, the Convention rejected the MFDP challenge and seated the white "regulars." Although the national party offered the MFDP two "at-large" delegates and promised to revise its rules to ensure that blacks were fairly represented in the future, SNCC regarded this compromise as an act of perfidy. It confirmed SNCC's suspicion that the northern liberals who controlled the Democratic party were as bad as the southern segregationists.

In a society as deeply racist as America, SNCC concluded, integration was a chimera. Instead of making futile appeals for assimilation into the white mainstream, blacks ought to organize themselves, developing their own collective power through racial unity, separate institutions, and independent leadership.

As a slogan, however, King thought Black Power divisive and ill-considered; as a program, he considered it confused, illogical, and vacuous. He had no quarrel with calls for racial pride, the amassing of political strength, or the pooling of black economic resources, and he recognized that the civil rights movement had placed too much emphasis on integration, neglecting more pressing economic concerns. But he dismissed as a delusion the notion that blacks could isolate themselves from white society, pursuing a separatist path to freedom and equality. And he deplored the ugly, irrational attitudes that Black Power encouraged. Despite their attempts to distinguish separatism from racism, advocates of Black Power increasingly articulated dislike of and contempt for all whites, and by 1967 antiwhite diatribes had become a standard feature of black political discourse. Stokely Carmichael, SNCC's chairman, popularized the abusive term "honky"; author Julius Lester wrote a best-selling polemic whose title, *Look Out, Whitey! Black Power's Gon' Get Your Mama!*, accurately summarized its sentiments. Both SNCC and CORE expelled their few remaining white staff members. It was not uncommon for black activists to cease, literally, speaking to whites.

The most damaging aspect of Black Power, in King's view, was its "unconscious and often conscious call for retaliatory violence." SNCC argued that in throwing nonviolence overboard, it was not so much embracing violence as affirming the right of self-defense and rejecting the tactics of nonviolent direct action. Certainly, SNCC made no serious attempt to initiate violence, and its advocacy of revolution remained purely verbal. Even the Black Panthers, the most quasi-militaristic of the Black Power groups to emerge in the late 1960s, stayed within the limits of armed self-defense. By and large, the debate over violence remained on the level of rhetoric. Even so, Black Power fostered a cult of violence that, even if expressed in words and not deeds, was in King's view fraught with danger. Dignifying the ghetto riots as political revolts encouraged further rioting. It confused the legitimate right of self-defense with the very different issue of carrying arms during demonstrations, a practice King considered suicidal. It glamorized violent revolution, implanting dangerous fantasies in the minds of young blacks. By alarming whites, it strengthened the hand of the right wing, making blacks more vulnerable to preemptive violence by the white authorities.[8]

The appeal of Black Power, however, transcended political logic. Blacks thrilled to the slogan's boldness and applauded the bravado of its propagandists. By 1966 King's talk of love seemed cringingly deferential and embarrassingly naïve. Blacks across America embraced Black Power as a psychological liberation, a symbolic, black Declaration of Independence. In substituting the word "black" for "Negro," the slogan rejected the elitism of the black upper class, which prized light skin and European features, and attacked the negative self-image that still prompted many blacks to deemphasize their African characteristics. Stressing the word "power" seemed more attuned to the harsh realities of America than King's "dream" of a "beloved community". Joining the two words together challenged the notion that black progress depended upon white goodwill, and placed blacks on a par with the Irish, the Jews, and other ethnic groups. In spurning white allies Black Power insisted that blacks would choose their own leaders and formulate their own strategies, regardless of their acceptability to whites. In stressing racial pride, Black Power became a celebration of black culture and "soul," a quest for self-identity that stimulated a creative outburst in music, fashion, literature, and art. Its very ambiguity enhanced the slogan's appeal: it seemed to offer something to everyone.

When SNCC raised the cry of Black Power, however, the semblance of black unity disappeared in a welter of invective. Roy Wilkins of the NAACP denounced Black Power as "a reverse Mississippi, a reverse Hitler, a reverse Ku Klux Klan." SNCC and CORE ridiculed Wilkins as an aging Uncle Tom and dismissed the NAACP as a pathetic caricature of the white bourgeoisie. King attempted to restore unity, but the chasm between Black Power advocates and integration-minded traditionalists proved unbridgeable. Moreover, King's Vietnam speeches had damaged his standing with conservative blacks, many of whom blamed him for creating an impression that blacks were unpatriotic. A few suspected that Communists were manipulating King, and that, as one NAACP official put it, "leftists, peace-niks, militants, and other oddballs" were trying to infiltrate the civil rights movement.[9]

By 1967 the civil rights movement had disintegrated. When SNCC and CORE embraced Black Power their white financial support all but evaporated; the organizations that had been on the cutting edge of black protest declined into insignificance. SCLC survived, but having left the South it was still having difficulty taking root in the North. Repudiated by left and right, King felt increasingly isolated. For the first time in six years, he failed to lead a campaign of nonviolent direct action. People expected him to have answers, he told his wife, but he had none.

King stated many times that Vietnam had become the major roadblock to reform. He feared that America was gripped by a "war psychosis," which, added to the atmosphere of white paranoia fostered by ghetto rioting and Black Power, threatened a recrudescence of McCarthyism and the advent of right-wing, authoritarian governments. Practical considerations, however, dissuaded King from making Vietnam his overriding concern. The amorphous peace movement remained divided on both strategy and tactics, and King's initial hope that he could emerge as the leader of a united front quickly faded. While continuing to attack the war, he had reservations about the provocative and sometimes bizarre tactics of the New Left and worried that if he became too involved with the predominantly white peace movement he would become estranged from his black constituency. Ending the war, he realized, would take time. It demanded a political strategy to "dump Johnson" as the Democratic candidate in 1968. In the meantime the ghettos were becoming a war zone. No sooner had the 1967 outbreaks subsided than the nation began steeling itself for the next "long, hot summer."

In October 1967 King unveiled plans for the Poor People's Campaign. In the following spring, he promised, a "nonviolent army" of three thousand poor people, to be recruited by SCLC, would build a shantytown in Washington, occupying public land within sight of the White House and the Capitol. And they would stay there indefinitely—for as long as it took to persuade the federal government to address the issue of poverty in a root-and-branch manner. If necessary, King warned, he would organize mass civil disobedience designed to disrupt the functioning of Washington.

It was a bold and novel venture. The Poor People's Campaign transcended ethnic and racial divisions, challenged the very concept of Black Power, and envisaged an explicitly class-based movement that questioned the verities of American capitalism. By raising economic questions in such a radical form, King consciously attempted to thrust democratic socialism—albeit couched in the language of the Social Gospel—into the mainstream of political debate. He avoided using the term "socialism," because, as he told Levison, Americans "respond so emotionally

119

and irrationally to it." But he frankly called for "poor people's power." The United States already had a long tradition of "socialism for the rich," he noted sardonically; the poor, in seeking an "Economic Bill of Rights," would merely be asking for what was theirs by right. King proposed to build a new political movement, virtually from scratch.[10]

His plans evoked opposition and skepticism, even from close friends and colleagues. His former theology professor, Harold DeWolf, cautioned that anything resembling an attempt to coerce Congress would strengthen the forces of reaction and might even provoke a "Fascist-type revolution." Bayard Rustin doubted King's ability to maintain nonviolent discipline: by threatening disruptive tactics he would attract "the most irresponsible and uncontrollable elements." James Bevel argued that ending the war ought to be SCLC's top priority: a campaign of resistance to the draft would mobilize young people and "get the war machine to attack us." If King mounted demonstrations in Washington, Bevel doubted that President Johnson would "give enough opposition for us to build up steam and momentum." SCLC's rank-and-file staff members felt confused about the campaign and found it difficult to persuade the poor to sign up.[11]

King responded by redoubling his efforts to mobilize support. Meanwhile, he was cheered by the results of the New Hampshire presidential primary election, in which Senator Eugene McCarthy, an antiwar Democrat, almost beat President Johnson. Four days later, Robert Kennedy announced his candidacy. "If there's any possibility of stopping Lyndon," King believed, "it's going to be Kennedy."[12]

On March 18, 1968, King addressed a rally in Memphis, Tennessee, to express support for the city's sanitation workers, who were striking for union recognition and a wage rise. Impressed that the black community, including the churches, was solidly behind the strikers—especially after the police had broken up a peaceful march using clubs and mace—he agreed to return. He promised to lead a march to city hall. His staff was annoyed by the diversion, but King reasoned that this was an issue that tied into the Poor People's Campaign and that the local mayor, Henry Loeb, exhibited an obstinacy and obtuseness that would play into his hands.

But the demonstration on March 28 was badly organized, and to make matters worse, a group of young militants who styled themselves "The Invaders" were bent on disruption, angry that the black ministers, especially James Lawson, had snubbed them. King arrived on the scene late to find people milling about in confusion. Shortly after the column set off, some blacks began to smash shop windows. As Lawson tried to restore order, the police decided to clear the streets, wading into the crowd with flailing clubs and firing tear gas at fleeing marchers. King was hustled away from the scene by his staff, who commandeered a passing car to drive him to safety. The governor of Tennessee sent 3,800 National Guardsmen into Memphis and imposed a 7:00 P.M. curfew. President Johnson offered to send federal troops.

Shaken and disconsolate, King was tempted to cancel the Poor People's Campaign. He even considered embarking on a fast in an effort to unite the black community behind his leadership. For the first time in his career, he had lost control of one of his own marches, and a sixteen-year-old boy had been killed by the police. Speaking over the phone, Stanley Levison tried to convince him that it was unrealistic to expect complete nonviolence, reminding him that in the 1930s labor unions had persevered with strikes despite the violence of agents provocateurs. This was entirely different, King replied. "Let's face it, this was a riot that broke out right in the ranks of our march." As the symbol of nonviolence, his reputation had been tarnished, perhaps irreparably.[13]

At a marathon staff meeting in Atlanta on March 30 King was persuaded to continue with the Poor People's Campaign, as well as to return to Memphis for a disciplined, nonviolent march. The following day brought welcome news: President Johnson announced that he would not run for reelection and would seek negotiations with North Vietnam. The political clouds seemed to be lifting, and King's spirits improved.

On the evening of April 3 King addressed a rally in Memphis, delivering one of the most powerful speeches of his life. "Like anybody, I would like to live a long life," he concluded:

> Longevity has its place. But I'm not concerned about that now. I just want to do God's will. And He's allowed me to go up to the mountaintop. And I've looked over. And I've seen the Promised Land. I may not get there with you. But I want you to know tonight that we as a people will get to the Promised Land. So I'm happy tonight. I'm not worried about anything. I'm not fearing any man. "Mine eyes have seen the glory of the coming of the Lord." [14]

The following evening, delighted that a federal judge had rejected the city's request for a ban on the march, he prepared to visit the home of a local preacher for dinner. As he paused on the balcony outside his motel room, chatting affably with staff members, a bullet tore into his face. Moments later King was dead.

8

The Man and the Legacy

ON FRIDAY, APRIL 5, 1968, President Lyndon B. Johnson ordered the Stars and Stripes to be flown at half-mast and proclaimed the following Sunday a day of national mourning. At the service preceding King's interment in Atlanta, a bevy of white dignitaries—mayors, governors, senators, Supreme Court justices, the vice-president—paid tribute to King in Ebenezer Baptist Church. With the exception of Robert Kennedy (soon to become another victim of an assassin's bullet), most of the whites looked acutely uncomfortable in this tiny integrated island surrounded by a sea of black mourners.

For large numbers of white Americans King's assassination evoked guilt and shame; many sought personal atonement in acts of generosity and goodwill. Whites donated money to SCLC in record amounts. A flurry of interracial meetings and religious services took place. On April 5 in Memphis three hundred ministers, white and black, marched to city hall in support of the striking sanitation workers, who finally won their demands eleven days later.

King's enemies for the most part celebrated in private. Former governor of Alabama George Wallace—the only presidential candidate absent from King's funeral—greeted the death of his old nemesis with pregnant silence. Other conservatives deplored the manner of his death while implying that King had brought it upon himself. Presidential aspirant Ronald Reagan, the governor of California, attributed King's demise to the fact that "we began compromising with law and order, and people started choosing which laws they'd break." According to the *Shreveport Journal*, "King should not have been stopped by an assassin's bullet but by the law." Such expressions of regret, however, often disguised a grim satisfaction. In taverns across America there were whites who toasted King's death. And in the FBI's Atlanta office, one agent could hardly contain his glee as the fist of one hand hit the palm of another: "They finally got the s.o.b.!"[1]

African Americans were well aware of the depth of white hatred for King, and many viewed the ostentatious mourning by the nation's leaders with cynicism. Spontaneously, obeying nobody's orders and without any common plan or purpose, blacks poured into the streets by the thousands. In a paroxysm of grief and anger that shook 125 cities, they fought with the police and smashed shop windows, burning and looting as they temporarily "liberated" the ghettos. Sixty-eight thousand troops—about a third of them regular soldiers—helped to suppress the outbreak. When the revolt subsided on April 11, forty-six people were dead, about thirty-five thousand injured, and more than twenty thousand in jail. All but a handful of the dead were African Americans. Some of the worst rioting occurred in the capital, less than a mile from the White House, where seven people were killed. "I remember the sick feeling that came over me . . . as I saw black smoke from burning buildings fill the sky over Washington," wrote President Johnson, "and as I watched armed troops patrolling the streets . . . for the first time since the Civil War." In Chicago, where rioting claimed eleven lives, Mayor Daley instructed his police to "shoot to kill arsonists, and shoot to maim looters."[2]

The 1968 Civil Rights Act, which Congress passed on April 10, was commonly described as a tribute to King. The act outlawed discrimination in the sale and rental of housing, and made it a crime to kill, injure, or intimidate people who were exercising their civil rights or encouraging others to do so. The Johnson administration had been pushing this measure for several months; commentators speculated that King's death might have swayed wavering members of Congress, but the assertion is impossible to prove. In any event, as a legislative victory the act was singularly barren. The ban on housing discrimination was virtually impossible to enforce, and the provision for protecting civil rights workers came at least four years too late. Moreover, the act had a sting in its tail: "Rap Brown" amendments (named after the SNCC leader who popularized the saying "Violence is as American as cherry pie") made it a crime to cross into another state or communicate between states, with intent to incite, organize, encourage, or participate in a riot.

For the poor, there was nothing redemptive about King's death. The government remained deaf to proposals for a crash program to rebuild the inner cities, let alone to guarantee full employment or abolish poverty. Congress was determined to slash spending on social programs as the price for granting the tax increase requested by President Johnson—an increase necessitated by the soaring cost of the war in Vietnam. Johnson, anxious to curb inflation, readily acquiesced. On March 2 the Kerner Commission, which had been appointed by Johnson to investigate the causes of the previous summer's riots, called for "unprecedented levels of funding" to produce "quick and visible progress" for poor people and racial minorities. Johnson all but ignored the commission's report, and the riots of early April made him even less disposed to support such proposals. The day after King's funeral, Johnson read a memo from a member of his White House staff urging him to address a joint session of Congress, as he had promised on

April 5, in order to request $5 billion for "quick impact programs." Writing angry, petulant comments in the margin, Johnson ridiculed the suggestion. Yes, he had intended to address Congress, but the riots had caused him to abandon the idea. As for more spending, "Forget it." On June 21 Congress approved a tax increase and lopped $6 billion from the federal budget.[3]

A few hundred yards away, the Poor People's Campaign petered out as the inhabitants of Resurrection City, SCLC's squalid shanty town, floundered in a sea of mud and crime. After King's assassination the Poor People's Campaign attracted levels of support it had never enjoyed when King was alive. During a few weeks in May and June, however, King's bickering, self-important heirs squandered this legacy in a campaign of astonishing ineptitude.

SCLC never recovered. James Bevel left the organization in 1969 and drifted into obscurity. Andrew Young departed the following year to become in turn a congressman, U.S. ambassador to the United Nations, and mayor of Atlanta. Jesse Jackson quit SCLC in 1971 and founded his own organization; thirteen years later he made his first bid for the Democratic presidential nomination. Ralph Abernathy, King's handpicked successor, presided over an ailing SCLC until 1977. SCLC still survives, but it has little influence.

Had he lived King would have found it difficult if not impossible to arrest the decline of the civil rights movement. Indeed, some have depicted him as a burnt-out case. In Andrew Young's view, King had developed unrealistic expectations of his own leadership, and the inordinate burdens he shouldered were becoming too much for him. During the year before his death, Young recalled, King slept little and found it difficult to relax; moreover, he seemed so preoccupied with death that wondering how and when it would arrive had become agony. David Garrow, King's most thorough biographer, believes that by the time of his death King had become exhausted, discouraged, and depressed.[4]

Yet, King might have achieved much more. For all his depression, King never gave in to despair. The apocalyptic tone of his later speeches was partly a calculated escalation of rhetoric. For example, a posthumously published article conveyed the impression that he saw the Poor People's Campaign as a make-or-break "showdown for nonviolence." But shortly before his death King had criticized the ghostwritten draft on precisely that score. The press had twisted his words, he complained, portraying the Poor People's Campaign as a desparate all-or-nothing gamble. King had more modest and realistic expectations of the campaign. As with Birmingham, he believed that even a small victory could have far-reaching effects: concessions from Congress might revive hope in the ghettos, blunt the appeal of black separatism, and halt the vicious spiral of rioting and repression.

Andrew Young believed that "Martin had done about all that he could." Yet Bayard Rustin testified to King's ability to "pull victory from the jaws of defeat," recalling "five or six instances I said, 'Martin, if you do that you are finished,' and he did it and got more prestige." For Stanley Levison, the shambles of the Poor People's Campaign revealed the true quality of King's leadership for the first time. "Now everybody realizes not only how important he was but also that he was a first-rate organizer." Even his critics recognized that King towered above other black leaders. For Stokely Carmichael, King was "the one man of our race that this country's older generations, the militants and the revolutionaries, and the masses of black people would still listen to." [5]

Ironically, the FBI shared Carmichael's assessment. On March 4, 1968, FBI headquarters had ordered a concerted campaign to "prevent the rise of a 'messiah' who could unify and electrify the militant black nationalist movement." King, it believed, "could be a very real contender for this position." The FBI's efforts to discredit King and to disrupt the Poor People's Campaign continued until the day he died and beyond. [6]

It was only after Hoover's death, and in the climate of moral indignation produced by the Watergate scandal, that the nation learned of the FBI's vendetta against King. The revelations of a Senate investigation in 1975 fuelled widely held suspicions about possible FBI involvement in King's assassination, helping to spur the creation in 1978 of the House Select Committee on Assassinations. Although the committee unearthed further shocking details of Hoover's efforts to discredit King, its final report acquitted the FBI of King's murder. James Earl Ray indeed killed King, the committee concluded; he had possibly been assisted by two brothers and may have been responding to a "standing offer" on King's life put out by two St. Louis businessmen. Many people remain unpersuaded, however. King's assassination, like that of President Kennedy, continues to generate conspiracy theories.

For such black militants as Stokely Carmichael, King's death confirmed the futility of nonviolence. "When white America killed Dr. King she opened the eyes of every black man in this country. . . . There no longer needs to be any intellectual discussion. Black people know that they have to get guns."

But the militancy spawned by Black Power was largely one of posture rather than action. Loose talk of revolution, moreover, merely intensified government repression. During the first two years of the Nixon administration local police forces and the FBI, given virtual carte blanche by the Justice Department, destroyed self-styled revolutionary groups through prosecutions, violent confrontations, and the infiltration of informants and agents provocateurs. According to one tally, the police killed twenty-seven members of the Black Panthers in 1969 alone. Carmichael, the high priest of Black Power, went to live in Africa.[7]

The failure of Black Power bred apathy and cynicism; black expectations plummeted. King's optimistic philosophy had underestimated the depth and durability of white racism, leaving blacks unprepared for sharp reverses and tenacious resistance. Black

Power's failure also exacted a profound emotional toll on the foot soldiers of the civil rights movement. King had not appreciated fully the physical and mental stress experienced by ordinary activists in the front line of the movement; he had become too remote from the daily realities of the struggle. The philosophy of nonviolence could not survive constant brutality from southern whites and repeated betrayals by the federal government. When churches were being bombed and civil rights workers murdered, King's pronouncements on love came to appear patronizing, naïve, and grotesquely inappropriate. People might defend nonviolence as a pragmatic necessity, but few shared King's belief in the nobility of suffering. A younger generation rebelled against the notion of arousing the white conscience through displays of self-sacrifice. In 1976 black journalist Roger Wilkins noted that "there is a virtual moratorium on Dr. King's kind of dreaming."[8]

Despite this disillusionment, few blacks dissented from King's canonization. The struggle to publicly honor King's memory became an important focus of black efforts to secure respect and recognition from white officialdom. Coretta Scott King led a campaign to make January 15, her husband's birthday, a national holiday. And in towns and cities across the land, African Americans petitioned to have streets named after Martin Luther King, Jr. Whites often resisted such requests—or grudgingly renamed a run-down street or inconspicuous stretch of out-of-town highway. "White folks can't stand riding along a street named after somebody black," commented a black minister in Griffin, Georgia, where the city council refused to name a downtown street after King. In 1986, after fierce opposition from a number of southern Senators, a reluctant President Reagan signed a bill that made King's birthday a national holiday. Several states, however, still failed to recognize the holiday or tried in some way to negate its symbolism.[9]

King Day was a gratifying victory for African Americans. Yet, the annual King Day celebrations are too often tedious and empty rituals. The endless replaying of "I Have a Dream" presents an insipid image of King that glosses over the radicalism of his message, the militancy of his methods, and the relevance of his life for today. Indeed, this smoothening of King's image began the day King died; white leaders and opinion formers, fearful of black violence, praised King the better to damn Stokely Carmichael, deplore rioting, and condemn Black Power. (Few detected the irony of using the dead King to lambast Carmichael—despite their ideological differences, the two men had been fast friends.) In death King became a symbol of national unity, a moderate reformer from the South, a foe of irresponsible militants—a thoroughly "American" figure whose achievements testified to the resilience of the nation's democratic ideals. The uncompromising opponent of the Vietnam war, the harsh judge of racism, the scathing critic of free enterprise, and the militant advocate of poor people's power had to be forgotten if King were to enter America's pantheon.[10]

Thus, the historical King has been smothered by portraits and panegyrics. Hagiographic biographies have eulogized him; in the retelling his life has become encrusted with godlike myths. King's references to death in his last speech, "I've Been to the Mountaintop," led people to speculate that he had experienced some kind of premonition of his impending demise—ignoring the fact that death and self-sacrifice had been a leitmotif of his oratory since 1956. In her memoir of their life together, Coretta King wrote that her husband, like Christ, had been destined for martyrdom "so that God's will and His creative purpose might be fulfilled."[11]

It is not surprising that King often seems irrelevant to a younger generation of African Americans. The rediscovery of Malcolm X, of which Spike Lee's 1992 movie biography is the best-known expression, is testimony to the seeming remoteness of King's image. Malcolm's popularity is also a sad reflection of the grim realities of urban life for many African Americans. Despite the growth of the black middle class, conditions in the inner-city neighborhoods have deteriorated since King's death. Black unemployment has risen steadily as factories and businesses relocate or cease operations. Racial segregation is more pronounced as whites have left the cities for the suburbs. Drug addiction has become increasingly common, especially with the rise of crack cocaine use during the second half of the 1980s. The homicide rate has soared to three times the level of the 1960s. A black "underclass" is now increasingly isolated from the social and economic mainstream of America. Since King's death, however, the white population has been distinctly unsympathetic to the problems of its poor and racial minorities. Instead, increasingly repressive criminal justice policies have doubled the prison population, with African Americans comprising about half of the nation's prisoners and about forty percent of the inmates on death row. It is hardly surprising that Malcolm X's acid indictment of white America and his scathing contempt for nonviolence find such a receptive audience today.[12]

Yet King's vision and example still inspire and energize. By exposing the injustice done to blacks, King helped to reveal injustices throughout American society. The civil rights movement helped to politicize Mexican Americans, Native Americans, women, and homosexuals. By challenging the conscience of the Christian churches King impelled the ministry, both white and black, to regain a sense of social responsibility and rediscover a prophetic voice. By confronting America with its most glaring political hypocrisy, he helped to revitalize American democracy.

King's most enduring monument can be seen in the South. Because of the civil rights movement, African Americans gained equal access to public services and public accommodations. They dramatically improved the quality of their schools, and some entered previously all-white universities. Many have found well-

paying jobs that had formerly been jealously monopolized by
whites. Blacks have also won a substantial share of political power.
African Americans serve as sheriffs, judges, county commission-
ers, city councillors, school board members, state legislators, and
congressmen. New Orleans, Atlanta, and Birmingham have black
mayors; an African American has served as governor of Virginia.
Today there are more black elected officials in the South than
in the rest of the United States. Poverty and discrimination per-
sist, and in the social sphere blacks and whites still lead largely
separate lives. But the old days of daily humiliation, systematic
oppression, and unrestrained brutality are long gone. The destruction of white supremacy represented an incalculable victory
for human freedom.

As befitting a man who regarded nonviolence as a univer-
sal ethic, King's influence extended and endures far beyond the
United States. In one of his earliest public statements, King defined the Montgomery bus boycott as "just one aspect of a worldwide revolt of oppressed peoples." Segregation, in his view, was a
form of "internal colonialism"; the civil rights movement and the
decolonization movements were related struggles against white
supremacy. King hailed the decline of European imperialism and
took a keen interest in the emerging nations of Africa.

Unlike W. E. B. Du Bois or Stokely Carmichael, however, King
never adopted a Pan-Africanist perspective. Writing in 1967 he
observed:

> Ghana, Zambia, Tanganyika and Nigeria are so busy
> fighting their own battles against poverty, illiteracy and the
> subversive influence of neo-colonialism that they offer little
> hope to Angola, Southern Rhodesia and South Africa, much
> less to the American Negro. The hard cold facts today indicate
> that the hope of the people of color in the world may well rest
> on the American Negro and his ability to reform the structure

of racist imperialism from within and thereby turn the wealth and technology of the West to the task of liberating the world from want.

In 1964 during a visit to Britain King called upon the Western nations to institute an economic boycott of South Africa and Rhodesia. By the late 1970s, the growth of the black electorate enabled such African-American leaders as Andrew Young and Jesse Jackson to shift American foreign policy away from its traditional support for these white minority regimes, contributing to the birth of Zimbabwe and the dismantling of apartheid in South Africa.[13]

It would be wrong to attribute too much to nonviolent direct action in the African context. Guerrilla warfare, not nonviolence, brought the white supremacists of Rhodesia to the negotiating table and led to black majority rule in the successor state of Zimbabwe. Guerrilla wars also helped to extinguish Portugese colonial rule in Angola and Mozambique. In South Africa, the most firmly entrenched of the white-supremacist regimes, blacks and coloreds staged boycotts and demonstrations throughout the 1950s. By 1960, however, state repression had become so severe that nonviolent direct action ceased to be a viable option. In 1961 the African National Congress (ANC) launched a campaign of armed struggle. When a Black Consciousness movement appeared in 1969, it seemed closer in spirit to the Black Power philosophy of Malcolm X and Stokely Carmichael than to the Christian nonviolence of Martin Luther King.

By the 1980s, however, interest in King and nonviolent direct action revived in South Africa. With the disastrous failure of the ANC's campaign of violence, blacks turned again to strikes, boycotts, and demonstrations. After the suppression of black political organizations, the Christian churches became a mainstay of the freedom struggle. The two leading church-based opponents of apartheid, Bishop Desmond Tutu and the Reverend Allan H. Boesak, had reservations about Gandhian nonviolence, but they admired and were influenced by King.[14]

King has been widely admired in Europe as well. In Britain, for example, Christian pacifists and "ban the bomb" campaigners, from the 1950s to the 1980s, have invoked King's example in their crusade to eliminate nuclear weapons. King also stirred Britain's black population and helped to spark a debate over racism that resulted in the passage of antidiscrimination laws modeled on those of the United States. In Northern Ireland the Catholic minority consciously emulated the tactics of America's civil rights movement when in 1968 they launched a movement to protest against Protestant discrimination. A little more than twenty years later, movements of mass nonviolent action succeeded in toppling the Communist regimes of Eastern Europe and breaking down the Berlin Wall. With the exception of Romania, there was little violence or bloodshed.

To some extent King has become all things to all people. When they comb through his writings and speeches, liberals find a moderate reformer; conservatives, an exponent of American ideals; radicals, a democratic socialist; pacifists, a follower of Gandhi; intellectuals, a scholar and philosopher.

In recent years, however, students of King have stressed that the black church, with its gospel of freedom and rich preaching tradition, formed the bedrock of King's values and leadership. The moral lessons that King drew from his study of white philosophers and theologians merely confirmed and deepened the beliefs that he had already formed as an African-American Christian in the bosom of his father's church. Even nonviolence accorded with a religious truth already familiar to him: the practical expression of Christianity "is that freedom lies in action, love in giving, and living in laying down one's life for others." The example of Christ

and the theology of the African-American church supplied King
with his paramount values.[15]

Hence, it is an error to regard King as an original thinker. As
he himself was the first to admit, the pressures of work made him
intellectually stale. There is little sense of development in his published writings, many of which were wholly or partly ghostwritten.
His statements on nonviolence do not reveal the searching, subtle
mind of Gandhi, for example.

Yet, as Keith D. Miller has argued, the lack of originality in
King's thought should not be regarded as a weakness. King's
ability to influence black Americans depended on the spoken
word, not the written one. And the power of King's preaching
lay in the familiarity of his language to his audience; by continually repeating certain basic moral truths and by borrowing
well-known quotations and examples, King made his arguments
inspiring and accessible. King's sermons and speeches were not
particularly intellectual and not especially original, but they were
masterpieces of popular preaching and democratic communication. King was in a league of his own as a public speaker—he
knew every device of the orator's art and could adapt his style
to different audiences, yet he always managed to convey complete sincerity. With relentless energy and dedication he made
direct contact with millions of Americans, whites as well as blacks,
through pulpit and lectern.[16]

His abilities as a preacher enabled King to articulate the religious enthusiasm and sense of moral certainty that many see as
the driving force of the civil rights movement. Religious faith was
crucial to King himself; as David J. Garrow has argued, King
came to view his leadership in providential terms. In the chaotic
turmoil of the moment, buffeted by forces beyond his control,
faith alone enabled him to make sense of his predicament and to
persevere. When called upon to make sacrifices, go to jail, and

confront death, the example of Christ on the cross was always before him.[17]

Some think that King's influence on the civil rights movement has been exaggerated. Andrew Young considered King to be unassertive and indecisive, and claimed that King and his close colleagues functioned as a team of equals. To Roy Wilkins of the NAACP, King was merely a "Great Exhorter"—a man who gave pep talks to the troops but did not actually command them. To SNCC, King gained undeserved fame by capitalizing on its own work in organizing local black communities. King himself acknowledged that he built upon the work of local activists; he disavowed any desire to dominate the movement. In Bayard Rustin's view, much of King's influence derived from the stupidity of southern whites, who were always making a martyr of him. From these perspectives, then, King fulfilled a largely symbolic role that did not require great organizational or tactical skill.

Yet King was more than a figurehead. He inspired not only by the word but also by the deed. "His life," one scholar has written, "was perhaps his most important public statement and his most profound word." King was a man of action. Cynics sneered that he went to jail "only" thirteen times and spent just thirty-nine days behind bars, but that misses the point: King was the first black leader of any stature deliberately to invite arrest while seeking out and confronting the most vicious southern racists. Risking death became a way of life; it was a principle of his leadership. That alone gave him a prestige accorded no other.[18]

King's less obvious leadership skills must not be overlooked. He kept his followers at a distance—even his own staff regarded him as a remote figure—but nevertheless he had a remarkable gift for getting on with people of all ranks and stations. Despite continually reflecting on his own shortcomings, he accepted other people for what they were. He tolerated the arrogance of a James Bevel and the insubordination of a Jesse Jackson, overlooking their weaknesses in the hope of harnessing their strengths. As Stanley Levison noted, it was only after his death that people could appreciate King's skill in managing such fractious, egotistical, and sometimes eccentric characters. "Only a Martin King could get them to do creative work. Nobody else can." Only a King, too, would refuse to fire a staff member caught robbing SCLC's safe—believing, correctly as it turned out, that given a second chance the young man would make a dedicated worker.[19]

In his desire to promote unity, King was patient to a fault, ever willing to put up with criticism and even abuse if he could further the common cause, and always ready to engage in debate if he thought critics were open to rational argument. It is difficult to imagine anyone but King trudging along a Mississippi highway beside Stokely Carmichael as the latter spouted Black Power; debating nonviolence with a roomful of young gang members in a cramped Chicago apartment in the midst of a riot; or attempting, a week before his death, to win over the black militants who had the previous day wrecked his march.

King sometimes struck friends as naïve. Tough-minded advisors cautioned him against wandering into political minefields like Vietnam. "King should realize that he is dealing with the State Department and the Pentagon," Levison once complained, "and not some stupid sheriff in the South." Yet King's judgments often turned out to be right. He was closely attuned to public opinion, had a shrewd sense of timing, and complemented his idealism with a sagacious pragmatism. On Vietnam, for example, his estimate of the fast-growing peace movement proved more sound than that of his more cautious advisors: less than a year after he delivered his much-criticized speech, "Beyond Vietnam," public opinion had turned against the war.[20]

King's popularity with whites has always inhibited his appeal to black radicals. Without doubt, to some extent King was tolerated, encouraged, and even sponsored by white elites because the aims of the civil rights movement served the interests of those elites. Enfranchising southern blacks benefited the Democratic party; it also enhanced the influence of urban business interests in the South by reducing the power of white voters in the Black Belt. Similarly, desegregation helped to modernize the South's economy by removing obstacles to investment and growth. As Bayard Rustin put it, the civil rights movement "hit Jim Crow precisely where it was most anachronistic, dispensable and vulnerable—in hotels, lunch counters, terminals, libraries, swimming pools and the like. For in these forms Jim Crow impeded the flow of commerce in the broadest sense." When King adopted a radical agenda, however—raising the issue of economic justice and challenging cold war orthodoxy—former white supporters moved to cut him down to size. The president withdrew his favor; northern mayors attacked him as a troublemaker; the press wrote him off as a has-been; the Supreme Court upheld his 1963 conviction for "parading without a permit."[21]

The realization that he had overestimated America's commitment to equality profoundly saddened King, causing him to ponder new strategies for social and economic justice. Yet, in the confused, violent, and increasingly bizarre atmosphere of the late 1960s, when the word "revolution" was being bandied about with reckless disregard for reality, he kept his political bearings, tempering his growing radicalism with a robust belief in democracy and an unshakeable commitment to nonviolence. King appealed to reason, not passion; to ethics, not self-interest; to consensus and reconciliation, not racial and class animosities. King never abandoned his belief that the "Beloved Community" could be realized within history. In one sense, he conceded, the Kingdom of God "may be post-historical" because "it involves something that is not here." Yet in another sense the Kingdom of God "is right now, as an inner power within you," entailing "the final refusal to give up."

The private man remained hidden from public view. King's role as a symbol, spokesperson, conciliator, and diplomat demanded constant self-control; the face he presented to the world, except when preaching, was placid to the point of blandness. "King on the outside," one reporter complained, "seems the same as King on the outside—always solemn, always confident, convinced that there is a right way and that he is following it." Behind his self-composed exterior, however, was a man continually examining his motives, questioning his actions, debating alternatives, and agonizing over decisions. As James Lawson put it, "the tensions and antitheses were strongly marked on the inside." King never doubted the soundness of nonviolence. But when it came to translating that moral principle into practical politics he confessed to an existential uncertainty, exhibiting candor, humility, and humor that constituted rare moral strength. "I am still searching myself," he confessed. "I don't have all the answers and I certainly have no pretense to omniscience." [22]

Notes

1 *The Shaping of a Mind*

1 Walter White, *Rope and Faggot: A Biography of Judge Lynch* (New York: Knopf, 1929), pp. 234–36; Martin Luther King, Jr., "An Autobiography of Religious Development," ca. 1948, file drawer 14, folder 22, Martin Luther King, Jr. Papers, Mugar Library, Boston University. Hereafter cited as King, "Autobiography."

2 Clayborne Carson, Ralph E. Luker, and Penny A. Russell, eds., *The Papers of Martin Luther King, Jr.: Vol. 1: Called to Serve, January 1929–June 1951* (Berkeley: University of California Press, 1992), pp. 4–18, 109–11; Martin Luther King, Sr., with Clayton Riley, *Daddy King: An Autobiography* (New York: Morrow, 1980), p. 142.

3 Stephen B. Oates, *Let the Trumpet Sound: The Life of Martin Luther King, Jr.* (New York: Harper and Row, 1982), p. 14; King, Sr., *Daddy King*, p. 82.

4 Benjamin E. Mays and Joseph W. Nicholson, *The Negro's Church* (1933; reprint, New York: Russell and Russell, 1969), pp. 58–59, 249, 279.

5 Martin Luther King, Jr., *Stride Toward Freedom: The Montgomery Story* (New York: Harper and Brothers, 1958), pp. 86–89; King, "Autobiography."

6   Taylor Branch, *Parting the Waters: America in the King Years, 1954–63* (New York: Simon and Schuster, 1988), p. 70.

7   King, "Autobiography"; James P. Hanigan, *Martin Luther King, Jr., and the Foundations of Militant Nonviolence* (Lanham, Md.: University Press of America, 1984), pp. 75, 80.

8   See Branch, *Parting the Waters*, p. 87; David J. Garrow, "The Intellectual Development of Martin Luther King, Jr.: Influences and Commentaries," in *Martin Luther King, Jr.: Civil Rights Leader, Theologian, Orator*, ed. David J. Garrow, vol. 2 (Brooklyn: Carlson Publishing, 1989), pp. 441–43; Reinhold Niebuhr, *Moral Man and Immoral Society: A Study in Ethics and Politics* (New York: Scribner's, 1932), p. 252.

9   Lawrence D. Reddick, *Crusader Without Violence: A Biography of Martin Luther King, Jr.* (New York: Harper and Brothers, 1959), p. 7. The King Papers Project, which is publishing King's collected writings and speeches under the direction of Clayborne Carson, has established beyond doubt that King's Ph.D. dissertation, and many of his graduate essays, contain numerous unattributed quotations from published sources.

10 David L. Lewis, *King: A Critical Biography* (New York: Praeger, 1970), p. 28; King, *Stride Toward Freedom*, p. 213.

11 Branch, *Parting the Waters*, p. 93; King, "Autobiography."

12 Coretta Scott King, *My Life with Martin Luther King, Jr.* (New York: Avon, 1970), pp. 78–82.

13 King, *Stride Toward Freedom*, p. 19; David J. Garrow, *Bearing the Cross: Martin Luther King, Jr., and the Southern Christian Leadership Conference* (New York: Morrow, 1986), p. 42.

2   The Montgomery Bus Boycott

1   Garrow, *Bearing the Cross*, p. 50.

2   Branch, *Parting the Waters*, pp. 138–41.

3   King, *Stride Toward Freedom*, p. 62.

4   *New York Times*, 24 March 1956.

5   J. Harold Jones, "Statements in Response to Question as to Why the People in Montgomery, Alabama, Walk, March 15, 1956," in Preston Valien Papers, Amistad Research Center, Tulane University.

6   King, *Stride Toward Freedom*, pp. 137–38; Branch, *Parting the Waters*, p. 176; *New York Times*, 24 February 1956.

7   Garrow, *Bearing the Cross*, pp. 11–17; Branch, *Parting the Waters*, pp. 129–36.

8   Lawrence D. Reddick, "The Bus Boycott in Montgomery," *Dissent*, Spring 1956, p. 111; Sarah Coleman, interview by Anna Holden, August 1, 1956, Valien Papers; Anna Holden, "Mass Meeting, Holt Street Baptist Church," March 22, 1956, Valien Papers.

9   King quoted by Stanley D. Levison, interview by James Mosby, February 14, 1970, p. 9, Moorland-Spingarn Library, Howard University.

10 Holden, "Mass Meeting," Valien Papers.

11 C. B. King, interview by Judy Barton, March 15, 1972, pp. 29–30, Martin Luther King, Jr., Library, Atlanta; W. M. Lee, "The Bombing Episode," January 31, 1956, Valien Papers.

12 Glenn Smiley to Muriel Lester, February 28, 1956, Glenn Smiley Files, Fellowship of Reconciliation Papers, Swarthmore College (hereafter cited as FOR Papers); Smiley to John Swomley and Alfred Hassler, February 29, 1956, FOR Papers.

13 King to Bayard Rustin, September 20, 1956, file drawer 8, folder 34, King Papers, Boston University.

3 *Prophet of Nonviolence*

1   Lewis, *King*, pp. 13–14.

2   John H. Cartwright, "The Social Eschatology of Martin Luther King, Jr.," in *Martin Luther King, Jr.*, ed. Garrow, vol. 2, pp. 165–66.

3   Willie Mae Wallace, interview by W. M. Lee, January 27, 1956, Valien Papers; King, *Stride Toward Freedom*, p. 82; E. D. Nixon, interview by Judy Barton, January 1972, p. 28, King Library.

4   J. Harold Jones, "Statements in Response to Question as to Why the

People Walk," Valien Papers; Smiley to John Swomley, March 2, 1956, Bayard Rustin Papers, microfilm, Alderman Library, University of Virginia; Rustin quoted in Howell Raines, *My Soul Is Rested: Movement Days in the Deep South Remembered* (New York: Bantam, 1978), p. 49.

5 J. Mills Thornton III, "Challenge and Response in the Montgomery Bus Boycott of 1955–1956," *Alabama Review* 33 (July 1980), pp. 163–235; Robert Jerome Glennon, "The Role of Law in the Civil Rights Movement: The Montgomery Bus Boycott, 1955–1957," *Law and History Review* 9 (Spring 1991), pp. 59–112.

6 Smiley to William Stuart Nelson, July 18, 1958, FOR Papers.

7 Stanley D. Levison to Roy Wilkins, [September/October] 1958, Rustin Papers.

8 Levison, Mosby interview, p. 17.

4 *In Search of a Movement*

1 King to Rustin, September 20, 1956, King Papers, Boston University; Lewis, *King*, p. 109; Garrow, *Bearing the Cross*, p. 99; King to Allen Knight Chalmers, April 18, 1960, King Papers, Boston University.

2 Ella Baker, interview by John H. Britton, June 19, 1968, pp. 16–17, Moorland-Spingarn Library; Levison quoted in Jean Stein and George Plimpton, *American Journey: The Times of Robert Kennedy* (London: Deutsch, 1971), p. 108–9; Bayard Rustin, interview by Herbert Allen, July 27, 1983, Rustin Papers.

3 Garrow, *Bearing the Cross*, pp. 56–58.

4 Ibid., pp. 87–88; Lewis, *King*, pp. 82–83; Branch, *Parting the Waters*, p. 201.

5 King, *My Life with Martin Luther King, Jr.*, p. 179.

6 King to Jackie Robinson, June 19, 1960, file drawer 9, folder 1, King Papers, Boston University.

7 Adam Fairclough, *To Redeem the Soul of America: The Southern Christian Leadership Conference and Martin Luther King, Jr.* (Athens: University of Georgia Press, 1987), pp. 47–51. For Baker's

criticism of a lack of leadership within SCLC, see also Baker to Rustin and Levison, July 17, 1958, Rustin Papers.

8   King, *Stride Toward Freedom*, pp. 212–13; *Time*, February 18, 1957, pp. 13–16.

9   Rustin and Levison to King, n.d., file drawer 1, folder 29, King Papers, Boston University.

10 Rustin and Levison, transcript of telephone conversation, July 21, 1968, FBI Levison File.

11 Raines, *My Soul Is Rested*, p. 473.

12 King to Coretta Scott King, October 26, 1960, Martin Luther King, Jr. Papers, King Library.

13 Harris Wofford, *Of Kennedys and Kings: Making Sense of the Sixties* (New York: Farrar, Straus & Giroux, 1980), pp. 132–33.

14 Levison and Rustin to King, n.d., file drawer 1, folder 29, King Papers, Boston University.

15 Edwin Guthman, *We Band of Brothers: A Memoir of Robert Kennedy* (New York: Harper and Row, 1971), pp. 154–55; Wofford, *Of Kennedys and Kings*, 156.

5   *Confrontation: Albany and Birmingham*

1   Slater King, interview by Stanley Smith, n.d., pp. 12–13, Moorland-Spingarn Library; William W. Hansen, Field Report, July 7–27, 1962, Hansen Papers, King Library.

2   Raines, *My Soul Is Rested*, pp. 398–99; Laurie G. Pritchett, Summary Report, 1961–62 fiscal year, Albany Movement Files, City Hall, Albany, Georgia; Pritchett to Asa G. Kelley, "Albany Movement," October 19, 1962, Albany Movement Files.

3   King quoted by Levison, in Levison and unknown male, transcript of telephone conversation, August 3, 1962, FBI Levison File.

4   William A. Nunnelly, *Bull Connor* (Tuscaloosa: University of Alabama Press, 1991), passim.

5   Wyatt T. Walker, interview by Britton, October 11, 1967, p. 52, Moorland-Spingarn Library.

6 Martin Luther King, Jr., *Why We Can't Wait* (New York: Signet, 1964), p. 74; Levison and Clarence Jones, transcript of telephone conversation, April 13, 1963, FBI Levison File; King, *My Life with Martin Luther King, Jr.*, pp. 229–33.

7 King and Coretta King, transcript of telephone conversation, April 15, 1963, box 13, folder 2, Bull Connor Papers, Birmingham Public Library; Burke Marshall to Robert Kennedy, April 23, 1963, Burke Marshall Papers, John F. Kennedy Presidential Library, Boston.

8 King, *Why We Can't Wait*, pp. 76–95.

9 Recording of May 6, 1963 mass meeting at New Pilgrim Baptist Church, on *Lest We Forget*, vol. 2, Folkways Records, FD 5487.

6 *March on Washington to Selma*

1 King quoted by Levison, in Levison and Jones, transcript of telephone conversation, June 2, 1963, FBI Levison File.

2 Andrew J. Young, interview by T. H. Baker, June 18, 1970, p. 6, Lyndon B. Johnson Presidential Library, Austin.

3 *Lest We Forget*, Folkways Records.

4 August Meier, "On the Role of Martin Luther King," in *Martin Luther King, Jr.: A Profile*, ed. C. Eric Lincoln, (New York: Hill and Wang, 1984), pp. 144–56.

5 Scott A. Sandage, "A Marble House Divided: The Lincoln Memorial, the Civil Rights Movement, and the Politics of Memory, 1939–1963," *Journal of American History* 80 (June 1993), pp. 135–61; Martin Luther King, Jr., "I Have a Dream," August 28, 1963, text of speech, King Papers, King Library.

6 Lee C. White, memorandum on St. Augustine situation, June 26, 1964, box 6, Lee C. White Papers, Johnson Presidential Library; John Herbers, *The Black Dilemma* (New York: John Day, 1973), pp. 26–27.

7 David J. Garrow, *The FBI and Martin Luther King, Jr.: From "Solo" to Memphis* (New York: Norton, 1981), pp. 68–72, 102–4.

8 Ibid., pp. 40–43; Branch, *Parting the Waters*, pp. 208–12.

9 Garrow, *The FBI and Martin Luther King, Jr.*, pp. 107, 125–26.

10 Johnson quoted in Richard Gid Powers, *Secrecy and Power: The Life of J. Edgar Hoover* (New York: Free Press, 1987), p. 393; "Playboy Interview: Andrew Young," *Playboy*, July 1977, p. 75.

11 Garrow, *The FBI and Martin Luther King, Jr.*, p. 134.

12 Young quoted in Victor S. Navasky, *Kennedy Justice* (New York: Atheneum, 1977), p. 150; and Raines, *My Soul Is Rested*, p. 476.

13 *New York Times*, 3 January 1965.

14 King to Young, note from Selma jail, February 4, 1965, King Papers, King Library.

15 *Public Papers of the Presidents: Lyndon B. Johnson, 1965*, book 1 (Washington, D.C.: U.S. Government Printing Office, 1966), pp. 281–87.

16 Oates, *Let the Trumpet Sound*, p. 355.

7 *Descent into Chaos*

1 Alan B. Anderson and George W. Pickering, *Confronting the Color Line: The Broken Promise of the Civil Rights Movement in Chicago* (Athens: University of Georgia Press, 1986), pp. 183–90.

2 James R. Ralph, Jr., *Northern Protest: Martin Luther King, Jr., Chicago, and the Civil Rights Movement* (Cambridge: Harvard University Press, 1993), p. 149.

3 Anderson and Pickering, *Confronting the Color Line*, p. 253.

4 King, Speech at Frogmore, November 14, 1966, box 28, folder 26, SCLC Papers, King Library; Levison to King, April 9, 1965, box 14, folder 40, King Papers, King Library; Bayard Rustin, "From Protest to Politics: The Future of the Civil Rights Movement," *Commentary*, February 1965, pp. 25–31.

5 Harry McPherson to Nicholas Katzenbach, September 20, 1966, box 22, McPherson Papers, Johnson Presidential Library.

6 Fairclough, *To Redeem the Soul of America*, pp. 335–42.

7 Ibid., pp. 339–40; Garrow, *The FBI and Martin Luther King, Jr.*, pp. 180–81.

8 Martin Luther King, Jr., *Where Do We Go From Here: Chaos or Community?* (Boston: Beacon, 1968), pp. 44–66.

9 Roy Wilkins, "Steady as She Goes," reprinted in *Black Viewpoints*, ed. A. C. Littleton and M. W. Burger (New York: Mentor, 1971), pp. 295–96; Gloster B. Current to All Staff, June 21, 1967, box 2, folder 8, Harvey R. H. Britton Papers, Amistad Research Center, Tulane University.

10 Fairclough, *To Redeem the Soul of America*, pp. 357–61; Levison and King, transcript of telephone conversation, February 27, 1967, FBI Levison File.

11 Fairclough, *To Redeem the Soul of America*, pp. 362–64.

12 Levison and King, transcript of telephone conversation, March 26, 1968, FBI Levison File.

13 Fairclough, *To Redeem the Soul of America*, pp. 376–77.

14 Martin Luther King, Jr., "I've Been to the Mountaintop," April 3, 1968, King Papers, King Library, reprinted in Flip Schulke, ed., *Martin Luther King, Jr.: A Documentary—Montgomery to Memphis* (New York: Norton, 1986).

8 *The Man and the Legacy*

1 Lewis Chester, Godfrey Hodgson, and Bruce Page, *An American Melodrama: The Presidential Campaign of 1968* (London: Penguin, 1970), p. 35; House Select Committee on Assassinations, *Hearings: Martin Luther King, Jr., Vol. 6* (Washington, D.C., 1978), pp. 124–25.

2 Lyndon B. Johnson, *The Vantage Point: Perspectives of the Presidency, 1963–1969* (New York: Popular Library, 1971), p. 538; Mike Royko, *Boss: Richard J. Daley of Chicago* (New York: Dutton, 1971), pp. 164–65.

3 Joseph Califano to Johnson, April 10, 1968, box 56, HU2/ST1, confidential files, Johnson Presidential Library.

4 Garrow, *Bearing the Cross*, pp. 602–22.

5 "Playboy Interview: Andrew Young," p. 74; Rustin and Levison, transcript of telephone conversation, July 21, 1968, FBI Levison File;

Levison and Victor [?], transcript of telephone conversation, June 9, 1968, FBI Levison File; Carmichael quoted in *U.S. News and World Report*, April 27, 1968.

6   Garrow, *The FBI and Martin Luther King, Jr.*, p. 187.

7   Manning Marable, *Race, Reform and Rebellion: The Second Reconstruction in Black America, 1945–1982* (Jackson: University of Mississippi Press, 1984), p. 125.

8   Roger Wilkins, "After the Assenter," *New York Times*, January 20, 1976.

9   Hollis R. Towns, " 'MLK Parkway' Is a Back Street," *Atlanta Constitution*, September 12, 1993. In Arizona a Republican governor rescinded King Day as a state holiday. Virginia decided to honor Confederate generals Stonewall Jackson and Robert E. Lee on King Day.

10   Richard Lentz, "The Resurrection of the Prophet: Dr. Martin Luther King, Jr., and the News Weeklies," *American Journalism* 4 (1987), pp. 59–81.

11   King, *My Life with Martin Luther King, Jr.* (New York: Holt, Rinehart and Winston, 1969), p. 150.

12   William Julius Wilson, *The Truly Disadvantaged: The Inner City, the Underclass, and Public Policy* (Chicago: University of Chicago Press, 1987), pp. 20–62; Coramae Richey Mann, *Unequal Justice: A Question of Color* (Bloomington: Indiana University Press, 1993), pp. 202–3, 220–24.

13   King, *Where Do We Go From Here?*, p. 57.

14   Boesak wrote a dissertation comparing King and Malcolm X.

15   Hanigan, *Martin Luther King, Jr. and the Foundations of Militant Nonviolence*, p. 312.

16   Keith D. Miller, *Voice of Deliverance: The Language of Martin Luther King and Its Sources* (New York: Free Press, 1992).

17   David J. Garrow, "Martin Luther King, Jr. and the Cross of Leadership," *Peace and Change* 12 (Spring 1987), pp. 1–12.

18   Roy Wilkins, with Tom Matthews, *Standing Fast: The Autobiography of Roy Wilkins* (New York: Viking Press, 1982), p. 327; Raines, *My Soul Is Rested*, p. 56; Frederick L. Downing, *To See the Promised Land: The Faith Pilgrimage of Martin Luther King, Jr.* (Macon: Mercer University Press, 1986), p. 24.

19   Levison and Gloria Cantor, transcript of telephone conversation, June 7, 1968, FBI Levison File.

20   Levison and Harry Wachtel, transcript of telephone conversation, April 6, 1967, FBI Levison File.

21   Bayard Rustin, "From Protest to Politics: The Future of the Civil Rights Movement," *Commentary* 39 (February 1965), p. 25.

22   David Halberstam, "The Second Coming of Martin Luther King," in *Martin Luther King, Jr.: A Profile*, ed. C. Eric Lincoln (New York: Hill and Wang, 1984), pp. 202–3; King, Speech at Frogmore, November 14, 1966, SCLC Papers, King Library.

Bibliographical Essay

In spite of his short life, most biographies of King are substantial works, and each succeeding volume seems to get thicker. The earliest, Lawrence D. Reddick, *Crusader Without Violence: A Biography of Martin Luther King, Jr.* (New York: Harper and Brothers, 1959), is a valuable account of the Montgomery bus boycott by an African-American historian who took part in it. It also offers a surprisingly frank assessment of King's leadership. Lerone Bennett, Jr., *What Manner of Man: A Biography of Martin Luther King, Jr.* (Chicago: Johnson, 1964 and 1968) is a rather flattering portrait by a prominent African-American journalist. William Robert Miller, *Martin Luther King, Jr.: His Life, Martyrdom and Meaning for the World* (New York: Weybright, 1968), the first important biography published after King's death, is a sympathetic account by a white pacifist.

The memoir of Coretta Scott King, *My Life with Martin Luther King, Jr.* (New York: Holt, Rinehart and Winston, 1969), provides useful material about King's family, but is superficial in its treatment of the civil rights movement and conveys little impression of what King was actually like. Martin Luther King, Sr., with Clayton Riley, *Daddy King: An Autobiography* (New York: Morrow, 1980), throws additional light on the King family and the relationship between father and son.

A new standard in King scholarship was set by David L. Lewis, *King:*

A Critical Biography (New York: Praeger, 1970), a sober and reliable account leavened by excellent prose and stimulating insights. It was written, however, before many of King's papers and the records of SCLC were opened to researchers, as was Jim Bishop, *The Days of Martin Luther King, Jr.* (New York: Putnam, 1971), a volume vitiated by the author's antipathy toward his subject. Lionel Lokos, *House Divided: The Life and Legacy of Martin Luther King* (New Rochelle: Arlington House, 1968) is a right-wing attack on King.

Stephen B. Oates, *Let the Trumpet Sound: The Life of Martin Luther King, Jr.* (New York: Harper and Row, 1982) is the first biography to use the resources of the King Library in Atlanta; the result, however, is disappointingly superficial. Far superior is David J. Garrow, *Bearing the Cross: Martin Luther King, Jr., and the Southern Christian Leadership Conference* (New York: Morrow, 1986); this Pulitzer Prize–winning book is the best and most reliable biography to date. Garrow's earlier work, *The FBI and Martin Luther King, Jr.: From "Solo" to Memphis* (New York: Norton, 1981), is also essential reading. Another Pulitzer Prize–winner, Taylor Branch, *Parting the Waters: America in the King Years, 1954–63* (New York: Simon and Schuster, 1988), is the lengthy first volume of a projected two-volume work that combines a biography of King with a history of the civil rights movement. Adam Fairclough, *To Redeem the Soul of America: The Southern Christian Leadership Conference and Martin Luther King, Jr.* (Athens: University of Georgia Press, 1987) analyzes King's leadership within the context of his organization.

A number of books examine King's thought and intellectual development. The best are Kenneth L. Smith and Ira G. Zepp, *Search for the Beloved Community: The Thinking of Martin Luther King, Jr.* (Valley Forge, Pa.: Judson Press, 1974); and James P. Hanigan, *Martin Luther King, Jr., and the Foundations of Militant Nonviolence* (Lanham, Md.: University Press of America, 1984). Recent works have downplayed the influence of the white philosophers and theologians that King studied while at college and seminary, stressing instead King's roots in the distinctive theology and preaching tradition of the African-American Christian church. See, for example, Lewis V. Baldwin, *There Is a Balm in Gilead: The Cultural Roots of Martin Luther King, Jr.* (Minneapolis: Augsburg Fortress,

1991); and Keith D. Miller, *Voice of Deliverance: The Language of Martin Luther King and Its Sources* (New York: Free Press, 1992). James H. Cone, *Martin and Malcolm and America: A Dream or a Nightmare?* (Maryknoll, Md.: Orbis Books, 1991), emphasizes the similarities, rather than the differences, between the two leaders.

Those who wish to explore King's life more thoroughly should consult Clayborne Carson, Ralph E. Luker, and Penny A. Russell, eds., *The Papers of Martin Luther King, Jr.: Vol. 1: Called to Serve, January 1929–June 1951* (Berkeley: University of California Press, 1992), which contains an excellent introductory essay about the King family; and David J. Garrow, ed., *Martin Luther King, Jr.: Civil Rights Leader, Theologian, Orator,* 3 vols. (Brooklyn: Carlson Publishing, 1989), a comprehensive collection of published articles about King.

Useful background works include Harvard Sitkoff, *The Struggle for Black Equality, 1954–1980* (New York: Hill and Wang, 1981); Robert Weisbrot, *Freedom Bound: A History of America's Civil Rights Movement* (New York: Norton, 1989); Manning Marable, *Race, Reform and Rebellion: The Second Reconstruction in Black America, 1945–1982* (Jackson: University Press of Mississippi, 1984); Aldon D. Morris, *The Origins of the Civil Rights Movement: Black Communities Organizing for Change* (New York: Free Press, 1984); Jack M. Bloom, *Race, Class, and the Civil Rights Movement* (Bloomington: Indiana University Press, 1987); Clayborne Carson, *In Struggle: SNCC and the Black Awakening of the 1960s* (Cambridge: Harvard University Press, 1981); and Howell Raines, *My Soul Is Rested: Movement Days in the Deep South Remembered* (New York: Putnam, 1977; Penguin, 1983).

King's own books are still in print and can be read with profit. See *Stride Toward Freedom: The Montgomery Story* (New York: Harper and Brothers, 1958); *Why We Can't Wait* (New York: Mentor, 1964); *Where Do We Go from Here? Chaos or Community* (Boston: Beacon, 1968).

Index